About the Author

Terry Dillon has led a successful life in education as a headmaster in Nottingham, one of Her Majesty's Inspectors of Schools, and as an international educational consultant, advising national governments in Romania, Montenegro and South Africa. He was born in a mining village in the West Riding of Yorkshire, where he started to play the cornet. His military service was spent as a musician with the Band of Her Majesty's Welsh Guards. He began his teaching career in Skipton and now lives in the Cotswolds, where he is a member of Creative Campden and a governor of a Chipping Campden primary school, St Catharine's. His other books include 'Light Me a Candle,' The King's Beacon,' 'Quarry Lane,' 'A Long Way Home,' and 'Justice'.

Dedication

To Todd Masilela and his family – with my deepest respect.

Terence Dillon

AURORA, ME AND SOUTH AFRICA

AUSTIN MACAULEY
PUBLISHERS LTD.

A CIP catalogue record for this title is available from the British Library.

ISBN 9781786291622 (Paperback)
ISBN 9781786291639 (Hardback)
ISBN 9781786291646 (E-Book)

www.austinmacauley.com

First Published (2016)
Austin Macauley Publishers Ltd.
25 Canada Square
Canary Wharf
London
E14 5LQ

Acknowledgments

My thanks go to my wife, Aurora, without whom much within this book would not have been written, and to the many South Africans across the nine Provinces who helped and advised me during the time I worked in South Africa.

Contents

Chapter 1

Johannesburg and Kruger Park

It seems strange for me to be writing a book entitled 'Aurora, Me and South Africa'. I have never lived in South Africa and I have never stayed there for more than three or four weeks at a time. So why am I scratching my head trying to think why I should be writing about the country and what I should be writing? It may be that English is one of the eleven official languages of South Africa, which gives me a greater chance of understanding what is being said to me than was the case in Romania when I was working there, or also when I was staying in Sardinia, which led to me writing, 'Aurora, Me and Sardinia'. Certainly, I found the use of English in South Africa common enough to enable me to converse easily with people from different backgrounds, white, black and coloured, socially and within the framework of the educational courses I had been invited to lead.

However, it usually didn't take long for those sitting around a table with me at lunch or over tea to begin to leave me with the blankness I had experienced in Sardinia and Romania as they began to converse in

Afrikaans, Xhosa, Zulu or one of the other official languages unknown to me. My chances of learning any were less likely than my chances of learning Romanian or Italian, with which I have made very little progress. But I reckoned as long as English stayed in common usage in South Africa, it didn't really matter.

The offer of work in South Africa came to me as a complete surprise. Without my knowledge, a company, The Centre for British Teachers, for whom I had done a good deal of work in various capacities, had submitted my name and details, along with those of two other colleagues, to the South African National Department of Education. For reasons known only to them, the South Africans had chosen me. It may be that they recognised I had already worked overseas with some success – a four-year contract in Romania working with the Romanian Ministry of Education, along with a good deal of school inspection experience in England with Her Majesty's Inspectorate, the then recently created Office for Standards in Education (OFSTED), the Independent Schools' Inspection Service and the Catholic Education Service, most probably had some influence on their thinking.

No matter, I was asked to fly to Johannesburg and then go on to Pretoria in February 2000 to meet with officials of the National Department for Quality Assurance in order to discuss what help I could offer towards developing the quality of education throughout South Africa and help the Ministry of Education in its efforts to provide equality of opportunity for the children of all of its citizens, no matter their colour. I have to say, my knowledge of what had been happening in the recent history of South Africa made it a challenge I looked forward to with a good deal of excitement and also with growing fascination.

It wouldn't be difficult for anyone to imagine the anticipation quietly stoking the excitement I experienced as my plane, which I had boarded early morning in Heathrow, touched down in Johannesburg on my first visit to South Africa, a country still adjusting, socially and politically, to the freeing of Nelson Mandela, ten years previously and his retirement as President in the previous year. I had some knowledge of the broad terms of reference – they had been agreed between the South Africans and the Centre for British Teachers. The British Department for International Development also had an interest in what I was commissioned to do as it was sponsoring improvements in South African education as the country endeavoured to come to terms with life post-apartheid.

I had never been to South Africa and yet, like many Englishmen, felt I knew a good deal about it. The high profile of the anti-apartheid movement in Britain had raised awareness of the disgraceful treatment of the majority of people in South Africa through what became known as apartheid and had won over thousands of supporters, not only in Britain, but across the world. Its success had led to the cancellation of the planned visit to England of the South African cricket team in 1970, the eventual boycott of South Africa from world sports, the withdrawal from South Africa of the international banks and an international embargo on the importation of South African goods.

I also remember in my school days, before the emergence of the anti-apartheid movement took centre stage, joining with fellow sixth formers to express our disapproval of the way we understood the black and coloured people of South Africa were being treated. It was only with the freeing of Nelson Mandela that attitudes changed outside South Africa and the policies of foreign governments, along with those of the new South African Government, began to change radically.

Now, in the year 2000, just ten years after Nelson Mandela had been freed from house arrest and six since he had been elected President, I was being invited to play a part in the changes which were being envisaged by the South African School's Act of 1996, a measure which made it an offence for schools to discriminate in relation to which pupils they accepted. The Act confirmed the intention of the Government of South Africa, which, by the time of my arrival, was under the Presidency of Thabor Mbeki, Nelson Mandela's successor, to ensure equality of educational provision for all children. How else could I feel but intrigued and excited by what might lie ahead of me?

The invitation to provide advice to the South African National Department of Education arrived just as I was completing my contract in Romania. I had worked with a team of colleagues since 1996 on a project, 'Reform of Finance and Management of Education', which was led by an education management consultant, Doctor Alan Norley. My responsibility, along with John Everson, a former colleague of mine in Her Majesty's Inspectorate, was to help reform the country's school inspection system and train school inspectors.

The new post-revolution Government in Romania was keen to introduce a more supportive form of external evaluation of its schools and seek to ensure that the inspectors became catalysts for change. The movement in Romania was towards decentralisation and away from the suffocating system which had resulted from communism, a political period which had come to an end with the revolution and execution of Ceausescu in 1989.

In South Africa, the Minister of Education, Professor Kader Asmal, was anxious to ensure that every South African child, whether black, coloured or white, could have a worthwhile education and, in the spirit of Tirisano, he could rid the country of the unjustifiable inequalities which had existed under white supremacy.

When the two projects in which I was involved began, much remained in the education systems in both countries from pre-revolutionary days. It is not surprising, therefore, that the leaders of education in both countries were seeking change. They sought to use school inspection, or whole-school evaluation as it came to be called in South Africa, to ensure that all schools were giving all their pupils equal opportunities to make the best of their talents. They were determined to ensure that political change would lead to educational change and in doing so benefit their countries by enabling them to take advantage of the rich diversity and heritage of their people.

As for South Africa, a good deal of thought had been given to how the country intended to move forward in its aims to achieve equality of opportunity in education for everyone, from childhood through to adulthood, and to create a multicultural society blessed with nationally agreed values. The Government recognised, even several years after the release of Nelson Mandela, many institutions in education remained dysfunctional, significant inequalities remained in schools in relation to basic educational facilities and learning resources, and little had yet been done to overcome the unacceptably high levels of illiteracy amongst much of the population.

To deal with these problems, the Government agreed a plan, which was linked to the policy which was known as 'Tirisano', designed to ensure that education was properly monitored, evaluated and improved. Through well-organised evaluation the Government hoped to be able to identify strengths and weaknesses in the education system and indicate where responsibility lay when any shortcomings were revealed. The Government looked for regular reports on the outcomes of the evaluations so that the Provinces and the National Education Department could make an appropriate response and those in the community could feel action was being taken to help implement the promises of equality of provision and of opportunity.

My arrival in South Africa coincided with the beginning of attempts by the National Directorate of Quality Assurance, a Directorate within the Ministry of Education, to put in place an effective whole-school evaluation system. Officers within the Directorate believed that if the effectiveness of schools could be measured and any factors associated with the success or failure of schools could be identified, they could produce reports which would help the Government take appropriate action. In doing this, they believed the principles embodied in Tirisano could be achieved. It was to help in developing this effective system of evaluating schools that I was invited to South Africa.

One of the pleasures of working in South Africa was the opportunity it gave Aurora and me to become acquainted with a country about which we knew very little. We came to love what we saw of South Africa as we grasped the opportunities, when our responsibilities allowed, to visit some of its more notable attractions. For instance, on my first visit, when I was due to meet for the first time the key people from the Quality Assurance Directorate with whom I would be working to discuss how I might fulfil the terms of reference agreed for the project, I decided, late in the day, it would make good sense to fly out to Johannesburg with Aurora a few days earlier than the planned meeting. The attraction was it would give us enough time to make a visit to the game reserve at Kruger Park, north of Johannesburg.

My daughter, Alison, had already visited the Park and spoken with great enthusiasm about what it had to offer and so I felt it an opportunity not to miss. I knew that so long as I prepared thoroughly for my meetings in the following week with Todd Masilela and other members of the Quality Assurance Directorate in Pretoria, a slightly earlier arrival in South Africa and a visit to Kruger Game Park would not detract from what I might need to contribute to those meetings. My email to the travel agency, 'Welcome Tours', on the Wednesday before we were due to travel reflected the very late decision. It also drew the agent's attention to our need to be in Pretoria on the Sunday evening. It read, '*My wife and I are paying a visit to Johannesburg on Thursday. We should like to visit Kruger Park on Friday, Saturday and Sunday as advertised in booklets here in the UK. Our preference is to join a group and travel to Kruger on Friday morning and return to Johannesburg on Sunday. We need to be in Pretoria on Sunday evening.*'

I received a positive response from the agents. They could guarantee an interesting visit to the Kruger Game Park and arrival in Pretoria on the Sunday evening. Once I had shared the news with Aurora, I bought the flight tickets and we began to look forward to our first journey to South Africa with a good deal of excitement. It was only tempered by my recognition of the importance of my meetings with the Quality Assurance Directorate and the need to obtain a clear understanding of what the Directorate required of me.

The flight to Johannesburg went smoothly and, although it was a journey of about twelve hours, the line of latitude between the UK and South Africa meant there was little prospect of our experiencing jet lag. This was to be a factor from which I benefited on each of the occasions I visited South Africa, most notably on the day I was rushed straight from the airport by Todd Masilela to lead a course of forty prospective supervisors without having time even for a cup of coffee.

Once we had landed I became aware, for the first time in my life, that I was surrounded by far more black and coloured people than white. Why I gave it any attention at all I'm not sure, but, as my work in South Africa gathered pace, the experience was one which I became very used to. In fact, my relationship with those I came to train in whole-school evaluation, people who represented a wide range of backgrounds, became one of real friendship, typified by their jocular responses to my Yorkshire sounding vowels, particularly the 'u' sound, and my similar response to the especially long drawn out way in which they said one of their favourite words, 'Oh – kay…'

Once settled into our hotel, Aurora and I were keen to savour what Johannesburg had to offer. I thought it would be a good idea to have a map of the city and so went to reception, where a pretty, fair-haired white young lady was on duty. 'Why d'you need a map, Sir?'

'Thought we'd have a walk round the main streets of the city. It's our first visit to Johannesburg and if you could direct us to some of the most interesting areas it would be great.'

'Wouldn't advise walking, Sir. Could get you a taxi. You'd be a lot safer.' The use of taxis has never been one of my strong points – it could be something to do with being brought up in Yorkshire – but the look of disbelief in the eyes of the receptionist at my suggestion of walking around Johannesburg was enough. A taxi it would be. I was learning for the first time what I had heard only as a rumour back in England – parts of South Africa could be dangerous.

'Is that the only way we can see any of the city?'

'It's the advice we always give, Sir.' I looked at Aurora, who was standing beside me. 'What d'you think?'

'Why not? Remember, we're only here for today. But it's up to you. If you want to see Johannesburg it seems to be the best way.'

In response to my nod, the receptionist booked the taxi and our tour of Johannesburg began. As we climbed into the cab, the taxi driver advised us to keep our windows closed and doors locked, again implying Johannesburg was not a safe place. We did as advised.

The flavour of a big city persisted as we moved from one area to another, the taxi driver pointing out the various landmarks, such as Johannesburg fort and art gallery, but as I looked through the car window there were other things which interested me. I was again struck by the huge difference in what I was seeing to what I was used to. I don't know why I was so surprised at how different the street view was. Black and coloured people dominated the streets and we saw very few white South Africans moving among them.

All of it was strange to me. It was not strange to the taxi driver, however, who reiterated what the receptionist had said. 'Certain places you just don't go. Down that street for instance,' he said, pointing down a street which looked like any other street. 'That's Hillbrow. Not the sort of place you'd want to go, especially when it's getting dark.' I was flummoxed by what he was telling us. I'd lived in London and not always in the most salubrious areas. Although I knew I always had to be aware of what was happening around me, and on one occasion as I was walking through St. James' Park felt a stranger's hand in my pocket, I had never had as many warnings. He went on to say, 'When I drop you at the Carlton Tower in a few minutes, don't hang about. Go straight to the lift and the top of the tower.'

By top, he meant fifty floors above ground level. The Carlton Centre, built in 1973, was the tallest building in Africa at that time. I began to think we were likely to spend more time in the lift than on the terrace overlooking the city.

'Isn't it a hotel and shopping area?' I asked.

'Don't know anybody who stays in the hotel. This is downtown Jo'burg. It's a bit different to where you're staying in Sandton. I'll wait for you down here. Don't trust you having to walk anywhere or wait for another taxi.' Whether his comments were aimed at insuring he had customers for another paid journey or not, his comments didn't fill me with confidence as we got out of his taxi.

Our walk across to the tower entrance was one of furtive looks and nervousness. Once we had pushed through the outer door and were inside the building we were struck by the emptiness of what we took to be the hotel lobby. Bearing in mind the warnings we had been given, we headed for the lift as quickly as we could and began the journey up to the top floor.

We joined several other people on the terrace at the top of the tower, all of whom gave the impression of being tourists, and began to study what was around us. The view across Johannesburg from such a high vantage point was awe-inspiring. I wasn't surprised to see cameras flashing in every direction. It took Aurora and me a while to absorb what we could see, but once we were settled we sought to identify significant aspects of the panorama, using the map the receptionist had eventually given to me. We picked out the university, the Oriental Plaza, Ellis Park, the famous rugby ground, which I was to have the pleasure of visiting later in the project, and Constitution Hill. But we were constantly aware of the taxi driver waiting for us down below, a factor which ensured we could do no more than spend a brief period enjoying the view. We had not intended to spend much time, but as I look back on the experience, I suspect the nervousness which had been engendered by the regular warnings of danger meant we spent less than we had anticipated. Without knowing how to explain it or why I should have to, it was a relief to get into the taxi and back to our room in the hotel.

On the following morning, Friday, we helped ourselves to the hotel's breakfast buffet, excited about what lay ahead. We had talked long into the night about what we were likely to experience in Kruger, but our conversation was totally uninformed. Neither of us had visited a game park before and so we had no idea as to what to expect: where would we stay; what dangers were we likely to meet; had we taken the right anti-malaria tablets? These were the questions we had discussed and continued to talk about whilst awaiting the transport which was to take us to the game reserve. I don't think either of us foresaw any real danger – we were not about to take the trip on our own in a hired car, for instance, and as far as we knew we would be in the hands of experts.

Right on time we were picked up by a small coach in which we were transported along with half a dozen or so other tourists to the National Park. Aurora and I still didn't know what to expect but the chatter in the coach inevitably brought up images of lions and elephants and the prospect of seeing what were called, 'The Big Five'. It was a term new to us but on that trip we learned that the key to a successful safari was to see 'The Big Five', which consisted of an elephant, a buffalo, a lion, a rhinoceros and the most difficult of all to come across, we gathered, a leopard.

We arrived at the small lodge around lunchtime. It lived up to its billing as comfortable and welcoming. We put our luggage in the bedroom, had a good lunch and our guide, who seemed to spend a good deal of his life in the Park, proceeded to outline the programme. There would be a trip into the Park in the late afternoon when the animals were likely to be seeking the waterholes and feeding before resting overnight. For the brave, there would also be a night trip to observe the animals which came out during the hours of darkness. If we preferred, we could spend our night peacefully in bed and be taken out during the morning, afternoon and evening of the following day before being transferred to the coach for the journey back to Jo'burg (we quickly became used to the shortened form of Johannesburg) on the Sunday.

We decided the night trip would not give us a real flavour of the game reserve or of South Africa, though in my case bravery might have had something to do with it, as did the fact that I had to be fresh for my meetings on the Monday; and so we chose the day trip. But first, we had to ready ourselves for the afternoon and evening sally into a world about which we knew little more than we had read in the guide books.

After lunch we transferred into a four-by-four, which was the normal mode of transport when on a safari, for our afternoon and early evening tour. The experienced driver knew his route, even though he had to deal with diversions enforced by the flooded areas resulting from the heavy rains of previous days. Some of the streams running through the Park were flowing at speed, reminding me of the county of my birth, but the hot and sticky air prevented any further comparisons. The constant cacophony of bird song from what I took to be warblers, finches, larks and similar birds reminded me of what I had overheard being discussed on the coach. The more knowledgeable had said there were up to five hundred different varieties of birds in the game park. It's amazing how you can often learn as much from chattering people and chattering birds as you can from a guide book!

Our driver did all we had expected of him. He was a fount of information and had us looking up, down, left and right as he pointed out what he thought might be of interest to us. When he saw what he called a bateleur eagle hovering and then diving to snatch up what looked like a mouse, he drew our attention to it, and did the same when he saw a group of egrets standing in a pool just off the road. He also pointed out a vulture sitting contentedly on the bare branch of a tree, its prominent yellow beak signifying the threat it could be to small scampering animals and the meaty remnants of bodies left by earlier assailants. It was a clear reminder to both Aurora and me of how harsh life could be for different animals, whether small or large, in the wild.

In the evening, the same driver took us on what he had described as our mystery trip. It was still light and we had good views of whatever he pointed out. We had regular sightings of what I thought to be deer but which he called impala, animals which skipped in and out of the bush grass in groups, seemingly nervous about what voracious animal might attack them. They looked to be the innocents of the wild, prey to many other animals which felt like a good meal. The driver pointed out a yellow billed stalk, a hornbill, a crested barbet and the large nest of a hamerkop. We also saw a horned antelope and something I didn't expect to see wandering around in the bush, an ostrich.

Eventually, our second journey into the wilds of Kruger came to an end and we returned to the lodge, a good meal and then bed in readiness for our second day. The intention was that we would be rising early to enjoy a morning's trip into the park and perhaps see all of the 'Big Five'.

The following morning, early, we continued our tour of the Park. Our expert driver knew where to go and before long he had us looking at a couple of young elephants, their horns entangled, fighting in front of the herd of much larger and older beasts, which seemed unconcerned about the youngsters and content to use their trunks to reach up and to feed from the foliage of the trees. Eventually, when the two young elephants seemed to have settled their differences and the older beasts had satisfied their hunger, the herd made as if to cross the road in front of us. It was only when the leader of the herd, a large bull elephant, turned and began to move towards us, its ears flapping and its trunk swishing from side to side that our driver decided it wise to back down the road, saying 'You'll be pleased to know that there are occasions when a bull elephant'll seek to protect the herd by attacking anything it imagines might be a threat. I think, by the way, this one's looking at us! We've an elephant which sees the wagon as a threat. Anybody want to stay and see if what I'm saying's true?'

'Not likely,' was the chorus of responses, followed by sighs of relief as the elephant, a huge animal which would have crushed the four-by-four and those of us in it with feet which looked the size of a small tank, decided it had given us an appropriate warning. As the vehicle backed down the rough track, it gave out a huge threatening bellow and then turned to continue to lead the herd through the bush. The elephant didn't know it, but that was the first of our 'Big Five'.

When the elephants had moved on, we continued our tour. Further down the road the driver pointed out a herd of buffalo as they moved across the open country at speed. Whether they were being threatened or not we couldn't see but could guess. 'There are so many marauders in the bush. The buffalo always have to be ready to run for it. Staying together, they hope they're not the one chosen for dinner,' the driver said with a laugh. For those of us not used to the ways of the ferocious animals of the jungle, it didn't seem a laughing matter. But we discovered almost immediately he wasn't wrong. A pack of wild dogs, seemingly unconcerned by our presence, came into sight. They obviously had the scent of a good meal as they stalked their prey, a large buffalo which had been detached from the herd. The way they created a semi-circle, as if to shepherd their quarry into a cul-de-sac before pouncing, was fascinating to newcomers like us. Our driver commentated throughout, saying that the dogs were the fiercest of all the predators because of their habit of hunting in packs. Thank goodness we never saw the outcome of their endeavours, or what happened to the buffalo they were stalking, but their intent was clear enough to convince us the buffalo was unlikely to be around for us to see on our return to the hostel.

A little further on the driver drew our attention to zebra, standing quietly in the distance, a fierce, scruffy, blood-stained jackal and a couple of giraffe successfully feeding from a tall tree. I suspect no other animal would have the neck and legs capable of doing something similar, though our earlier observation of the elephants indicated they tried. At one stage the driver stopped the car to allow us to look at a huge rhinoceros, its eyes peering at us through the bush behind which it was standing with as much interest in us as we had in it. It was the third of our 'Big Five'.

We were definitely in learning mode when it came to much of what the driver pointed out. Before the afternoon's tour was finished my eyes and neck began to ache as I peered from one side to the other to see something of fascinating interest, trying to take in as much as I could. All of it was so new and strange to me and I knew from the look on her face that Aurora was having a similar experience.

So far, we had seen three of the 'Big Five'. We had yet to see the most difficult to find, the leopard, the one we all wanted to see, and a lion. Eyes were pinned on the ground and on the boughs of trees as we searched for the spotted animal. And then the driver said, 'It sounds as though we're in luck.' One of his colleagues, another guide, stopped his truck by us and, pointing back in the direction from which he had come, he said he and his party had just passed a leopard resting on the branch of a tree a little further down the road. If we were quick we may have the same privilege. Our driver pushed on at speed but by the time we reached the appointed place the leopard had gone. The branch was empty. The leopard had obviously decided to move on. Disappointment all round in the four-by-four as the cameras disappeared back into their covers.

But it was just at the point where the driver turned the four-by-four that I had my thrill of the day. I spotted lions. There was a family of them in the tall grass by the roadside. 'Stop, stop,' I shouted to the driver and he obliged. I was the only one who had seen them and feeling as though I had won an Olympic medal I called out to the driver, 'Lions. Look. In the grass on the roadside.'

He responded immediately and backed the four-by-four so we could take a good look at the animals which we humans regard as kings of the jungle. They showed nonchalant interest in us as we sat safely in our four-by-four, hardly raising their heads to look. I assumed they were so used to seeing such sights that another truck, even though it contained Aurora and me, was no more than an uninteresting bore. For our part, we, and most others in the truck, were able to photograph a scene which we would share with family and friends for years to come. The lions - a lioness, a lion and two sleeping cubs - remained as they were, calm and seemingly contented.

It was the activity on the vehicle which reflected most signs of excitement. Out came the cameras and travellers who had been content to sit and observe were suddenly on their feet moving in one direction and then another, impervious as to what anyone else was doing, so as to get the best angle for a photo. Not surprisingly, however, the activity did not result in anyone seeking an even better view by taking the chance to step out of the four-by-four, even if the driver had allowed it.

And so, we had seen our fourth of the 'Big Five', a family of lions. But the leopard remained a mystery. The driver took us a little further in the hope of spotting the fifth of the 'Big Five', but we didn't have the bit of luck we needed. Nevertheless, we had had a great day and many memorable moments. What we had seen coloured our journey back to Johannesburg as Aurora and I described to one another what we had made of our experience. What was an interesting conversation continued as our driver followed the road to our hotel in Pretoria.

Throughout our journey from Kruger back to Johannesburg, another interesting aspect of South Africa came to light. We were struck by the number of black people we saw walking on the roadside. As there were no villages in sight, neither behind nor in front of them, we could have assumed their walk to be aimless. But the bus driver informed us they were mostly farm labourers heading either towards or away from one of the huge white-owned farms, the fields of which extended over several miles. 'You've to be careful when driving,' he added. 'They can be very difficult to see when it's getting dark, especially if they wear dark clothes. Their black faces don't show up when it's dark as easily as white ones. You occasionally see a body on the side of the road.' The matter of fact way in which he said it helped to create images of what life must really have been like in pre-Mandela days, especially when he pointed out, without any apparent sign of sympathy, a place on the road where he said he had seen the outcome of such an accident. It was pretty obvious attitudes had still a long way to go before they changed sufficiently to see all South Africans as equals.

Chapter 2

The Project

As I mentioned earlier, I had spent some time in Romania working with those in that country who were seeking to update the national system of inspection, a system which bore many of the characteristics that were present in South Africa before the presidency of Nelson Mandela. The centralised system which had existed under Communism prevailed, with the inspectorate continuing to see its role as an instrument of central control rather than a partner with schools in seeking educational improvement. It was the desire of the Romanian Government to change this approach which had resulted in my being invited into the country.

I had been very fortunate to have, throughout most of the sessions I conducted with the Romanian inspectorate, Aurora as my interpreter. I say very fortunate because our relationship extended, in due course, and for reasons I have written about elsewhere, beyond that of consultant and interpreter and led to our eventually becoming man and wife.

My good fortune extended beyond even that, however. Aurora's time with me in Romania meant she had a key understanding of the way I worked and of the messages on school evaluation I was seeking to share. As a result, she could and did become a significant support in South Africa, where she ensured course rooms were properly equipped, attended to the needs of the course members – sometimes there were as many as one-hundred-and-fifty – helped to prepare the course slides and checked that I had all I needed in the way of screens and projectors.

We both had much to learn about South Africa but a further strength Aurora added was an empathy with the recently franchised South Africans. As a person who had lived all her life under Communism, had been present at the time of the 1989 Revolution and the execution of Ceausescu, and had seen her country endeavouring to come to terms with a different form of government, she had some understanding of the situation which faced the new South Africa.

As we worked and shared our thoughts on what we experienced in South Africa, we began to see how two such different countries, having been subject to quite different political systems and having resolved them in different ways, were facing up to the educational challenges of the immense political upheavals both had undergone. I have no doubt Aurora learned a great deal after 1989 as the controls of her earlier life gave way to a more open society after the political upheaval in Romania and helped to explain to some extent her understanding of the post-apartheid situation in South Africa. I suspect one of the most significant aspects of curricular change she experienced in the school in which he taught in Romania was in the subject of history.

There is little doubt that the control exercised by the Governments in both countries impacted strongly on what history was taught I remember Aurora saying, 'Once Ceausescu had gone, the history teachers in my school asked 'What d'we teach now?' Being a history teacher myself, I can imagine the scene and the issue, though I must admit I never saw a school history book in Romania or South Africa.

History is often the story of those who write it and in Romania it had been written by Communists for over forty years. No doubt, the black and coloured children in South Africa learned the white man's history from what was written, but had to rely on the oral history told by their parents and grandparents to learn about their tribal history. No doubt, those who were commissioned to write the new school curriculum would have to make important decisions about what history to teach, about what was written in the new school history books, and in all probability tell a different story of the past to that which had already been taught. The implications were as important to the white children as they were to the black and coloured.

On that first trip to South Africa I went to the National Department of Education to meet those from the Quality Assurance Directorate in Pretoria with whom I would be working. My general terms of reference had already been agreed, but I needed to discuss them in detail with the people with whom I would be working. It was agreed at those early meetings that, in consultation with the Directorate, I was to provide advice on a draft national policy for whole-school evaluation, and identify training needs for the National Quality Assurance coordinating officials, district-based officials and school management teams. I was also commissioned to formulate the details of a programme and manual for the training of those operating at different levels in the process of evaluating schools. It was also agreed that I would provide the means by which the external school evaluation system which was to be put in place could itself be evaluated. Some challenge!

As I have written previously, the Directorate was keen to ensure whole-school evaluation would improve the performance of all the country's schools. If I could produce appropriate materials, oversee effective training strategies and devise a secure system for monitoring the evaluations, I was advised I would be contributing to the South African Government's five-year plan to create a democratic and prosperous society. I couldn't help but think that the intention was an admirable one, but my experience in Romania suggested the target date was perhaps one which was somewhat unrealistic. Undeterred by the task, however, I hoped I could help them achieve their goal.

It was in these early meetings that I began to learn the complexity of the task in which I was becoming involved. I had accepted the contract with the Centre for British Teachers believing the approaches to improving school inspection in the different countries in which I'd worked would suffice in South Africa. In meeting with Todd Masilela and his immediate superior, Dr Nomsa

Mgijima, Chief Director, I learned that the task was to be very different from those in which I had been previously involved. From the start, it was made clear that the term 'inspection' and 'inspector', or anything associated with either, was taboo. The terms were too closely associated with the harsh, unsympathetic system imposed on schools by the previous apartheid Governments.

At the meetings I was informed that the National Directory of Quality Assurance, aware of the feelings of the vast majority of teachers and the teachers' unions to which they belonged, had already been through a process of finding more acceptable terms for what it wished to do. In line with the National Education Policy Act of 1996, the National Directorate had decided to use different terms for the monitoring and evaluation of education. As a result, the term whole-school evaluation came into use, as did that of supervisors. I agreed with the Directorate that I could work with the terms, 'whole-school evaluation' and 'supervisors', the replacements for 'inspection' and 'inspector', and that these were more likely to win over rather than antagonise teachers who were still suspicious of anything which bore the name or even the feel of 'inspection' or 'inspector', terms which, to most South Africans, would reflect some of the worst aspects of the old regime.

I learned several other things at those first meetings. A key element in whether or not the whole process of improving the educational experience of all children could succeed was the ability of the nine Provinces into which South Africa was divided could work together to agree and then implement a national system. Each

Province, I learned, had its own officials and each one consisted of a number of educational districts. The idea of districts brought to mind my experience of the local education authorities in England and the difficulty, on occasions, of encouraging them to follow common practices. I couldn't help wonder whether the same problem might exist in South Africa.

Another fact which I learned in those first few days of meetings was another feature of South Africa which I felt could lead to a disjointed approach to the national education policy. South Africa had three capital cities; Pretoria, Cape Town and Bloemfontein. I could only guess that such a split in the National Government, with Cape Town the legislative capital, Bloemfontein the judicial capital and Pretoria the administrative capital, would result in the different Provinces having a great deal of independence. It soon became evident to me that the officials of each Province would have to be converted into recognising the benefits of any proposed national changes if there were to be a commonly implemented national system of education. I began to realise it was likely that any national educational reforms would not necessarily be acceptable to all the Provinces and that they may need to be introduced into the different Provinces at different stages.

This desire to encourage the Provinces to convert to a national system was an important part of the National Board's plans and had been referred to in the 1996 Act, where it stated the monitoring and evaluation of education would be carried out 'in cooperation with provincial departments of education.' It was this clause,

I suspect, which led to my having to base training courses in different parts of the country. On one visit it would be in Gauteng Province with its capital Johannesburg, on another KwaZulu Natal with its capital Pietermaritzburg, and eventually Western Cape with its capital Cape Town, the last of the Provinces to fall in line with the proposed national system.

The third important aspect, and the one which had the possibility of being the most difficult, was teachers unions' approach to the proposed educational changes. A concern of the Directorate was the likely reaction of the teachers' unions to any system which suggested teachers were to be judged by some outside body which operated in the style of the inspections imposed during the time of white supremacy. We agreed, therefore, it made sense that during my earliest visits I should go to meet representatives of the teachers' unions in Mafeking in the North West Province and East London in Eastern Cape in order to discuss the new approach with them and allay any fears they may have that the new system would simply be an updated model of the old; one which the Directorate was sure they would be unwilling to accept.

I wasn't surprised to learn that the unions were keen to protect school staff from the invasive system that had typified inspection under previous Governments and looked for a policy designed to support and develop rather than one designed to instruct and control. At least one of the unions, the South African Democratic Teachers' Union (SADTU), was keen to see their own policy, which was associated with the development of a teachers' appraisal system (DAS), incorporated into whole-school evaluation, a desire I could not see being delivered within the framework of the whole-school evaluation policy as it stood and as the National Quality Assurance Directorate envisaged it. In their view, and also in mine, if teachers were not to feel threatened by external evaluation, any form of individual teacher appraisal would have to be separated from the responsibilities of those carrying out external whole-school evaluation and would be better handed over to the leadership in the school and a school's own internal evaluation systems. The appraisal of teachers and school self-evaluation did, of course, imply the need for training for those who were to carry them out, but that was outside my terms of reference.

On my first meeting with Todd Masilela, I learned I was going to be working with a man who, with his brothers, had played his part, as had many others whom I was to meet over the coming years, in the fight against apartheid. I learned he had visited Western and Eastern Europe in his efforts to raise money for the cause and had also been involved in organising, in Swaziland, resistance to the apartheid regime.

During our meetings, his and Dr Mgijima's commitment to whole-school evaluation became very clear. Their references to the Minister of Education's desire to fulfil the intentions of Tirisano, the plan for the state to rid itself of the last vestiges of previous white Governments and offer good quality education to everyone in South Africa, helped to clarify the task ahead. The Directory's recognition that equal opportunities in education would play a significant part in the whole process of change in South Africa was fundamental to its approach to reform. It fully supported the new Government's belief that one of the building blocks in the system designed to achieve change in South Africa was education and that a different form of school inspection, one which offered understanding and support rather than what it saw as the insensitivity and antagonism of the previous system, had an essential part to play. It also recognised that if it were to satisfy the general demand for quality for all in education, it must create a body which was able to provide a secure and effective system for monitoring and supervising the quality of its schools. It was this which led to the introduction of the policy which would be known as whole-school evaluation, the creation of a trained group of supervisors to implement it and the establishment of a national body with the authority to oversee it, the Quality Assurance Directorate.

The meeting clarified what was expected of me. I was to provide advice on the proposed new policy of whole-school evaluation; seek to ensure it would be acceptable to all stakeholders; identify training needs; provide a plan and framework for training designed to ensure its successful implementation; give guidance on a mentoring system to help those at national, provincial and school level who were responsible for implementing the policy; provide advice on how the implementation of the quality assurance system could be monitored and evaluated; and, based on the outcomes, what would be needed at national and provincial level to ensure that the system of education could be further developed. To achieve such a wide range of objectives, we agreed a programme which took into consideration the need for me to carry out a good deal of the written work in the United Kingdom, for instance checking policies and preparing training materials, and more practical work in South Africa, such as training, mentoring and evaluating.

My good fortune was that my work in South Africa helped me to get to know many different parts of the country. In order for the message of the whole-school evaluation policy to be explained to those who were still suspicious of its implications, arrangements were made for me to visit different Provinces each time I visited South Africa. In the earliest days of the project, it meant my making a further visit to the Province of Gauteng, as well as the North West and Eastern Cape Provinces. The intention was to discuss the implementation of whole-school evaluation and its likely impact. As a consequence, I had meetings with interested parties in Johannesburg, and with the unions and other interested bodies in Mafeking and East London. For me, journeying around South Africa and visiting towns I had only heard of was fascinating.

I took the opportunity in Mafeking, for example, to visit the local museum and have explained to me quite a different story to the one I had grown used to hearing in England. Baden Powell and British troops played their part in the defence of Mafeking during the two-hundred-and-seventy-three days' siege by the Boers in 1899, but the museum curator was very keen to impress on me the critical contribution made by black South Africans who were part of the Mfengu and Baralong Regiments. His argument was that without their support the British would probably have succumbed, and he pointed out museum pieces which supported his view. I must say, I found his different slant on the siege of Mafeking captivating.

The visits which the project demanded meant a good deal of travelling, usually by car and on occasions accompanied by Todd Masilela. It gave me a real sense of the South Africa seen by few tourists. The four-hour journey between Pretoria and Mafeking revealed the towns of Lichtenburg, Coligny and Ventersdorp, for example. The last, I was told by my driver, was one of the first settlements in the old Transvaal and a town out of which hundreds of black people had been moved in the 1960s and 1970s under the old apartheid system. Chris, who was driving me on this occasion, also drew my attention to Lichtenburg where one of the world's largest diamonds had been discovered, resulting in what he called, '*The ten-year diamond rush.*' Apparently, between 1926 and 1936 many South Africans were drawn to the area in search of riches.

The meetings in the different Provinces drew in a range of people, keen to learn about the new policy and, in some cases, challenge its usefulness. The meetings were important, however, in that they gave the Directorate and me an opportunity to explain in detail the intention of the new policy which was being developed. It was my knowledge of the 1996 Education Act, which I had studied in the early days of the project, which enabled me to understand the questions posed by the Provincial delegates and provide some of the answers they were looking for. Their frustration with the

National Government and its failure to provide adequate support for change was an underlying theme in all the meetings. The Provinces complained there was little evidence of any positive initiatives at national level and at the slow speed at which new resources were being passed on to the Provinces to enable them to implement the new system. During our meetings, delegates from various Provinces also indicated their frustration with the National Directorate. In their view, it had been created to oversee a national policy on school evaluation and ensure an approach common to all the Provinces, but in fact it was moving too slowly and had achieved very little. (Interestingly, the idea of whole-school evaluation had been muted in 1996 but little seemed to have happened since to convert the idea into a reality. A number of theses, written by students gaining their doctorates over the past few years, refer to the whole-school evaluation policy of 1996. In fact, the national policy as I know it and as it was presented for discussion by the Secretary of State for Education at the National Conference in September 2000 was only passed by the state legislature in 2001).

The Provincial meetings were attended by representatives from different districts within the Provinces as well as the union representatives, who raised important questions likely to influence thinking before the policy was eventually finalised. The Gauteng meeting was especially interesting as, to my great surprise, it emerged that the area managers who were present were already considering using an evaluation instrument they said was in use in Scotland. They had also had a one-day seminar on evaluation with a senior inspector from Canada.

It was also in the meeting in Gauteng that I learned something of the way responsibilities were delegated within the Provinces and the extent of the opposition from schools to the old system. Those in the meeting explained how the Provincial head office had responsibility for strategic planning and the monitoring of the implementation of provincial educational policies, which were not necessarily national policies. They worked through regional offices which, in their turn, managed the district offices which had day-to-day responsibilities for their schools. The representatives in Gauteng revealed how, in the mid-1990s, their Provincial inspectors had been refused entry into schools and where they persisted in trying to gain entry they were physically attacked and driven away. Such animosity displayed by teachers on those occasions still remained, they said, even five years later. Not surprisingly, the main question they wanted resolving and which was asked was, 'What is different about whole-school evaluation which is likely to avoid such reactions and which could possibly help to change attitudes?'

In Mafeking I heard of the Province's attempts to develop its schools and to give them what was described as 'self-sufficiency'. The district representatives favoured the move to a whole-school evaluation policy as long as it was designed to support school self-evaluation. They did, however, express concern about what they saw as insufficient structure within the

Ministry of Education to carry out the policy of whole-school evaluation. They were also concerned about the lack of strategies which were in place to help failing schools, 'Of which,' they argued, 'there are many.'

The meeting in East London confirmed some of the concerns expressed by the representative's counterparts in Gauteng and North West Province. Their main concern was the extent to which whole-school evaluation would be punitive rather than supportive and how well those carrying out the evaluation would be trained to gather their information through inter-relating with the school rather than seeking to control it. They identified some of the issues which needed particular attention: these included the need for schools to have development plans; the need to monitor more closely the presence of teachers and pupils at the start and end of the school day; the need to train principals and governors in their responsibilities (the Department of Education had issued a guide for governors in 1997, 'What Public School Governors Need to Know,' to help governors understand the Schools Act of 1996, but nowhere did it mention school evaluation as one of their responsibilities); and the importance of schools being helped to carry out school self-evaluations.

I understood the concerns being expressed by the Provinces and said so. I also recognised the importance of not antagonising them and sought to explain the evaluation policy as it currently stood and outlined what was intended in the way of organisation and training. I also drew attention to how important it was to bring together the information gathered about the schools in the different Provinces into a single report which could be passed on to the Government and help them to see what changes were required. I added that hopefully the Government would respond to their needs and listen to their concerns.

When socialising with the Provincial representatives after the meetings I had the feeling of a positive response from those with whom I spoke. Their main worries were not surprising. They were anxious to have their concerns heard by the authorities and that this should result in their receiving backing from the Government in their efforts to improve educational provision. They looked for assurances from the Government that it would respond to the outcomes of whole-school evaluation, and from me that the training of the supervisors would be of good quality. 'Only if supervisors are well trained and seen as supportive of the work of schools, providing appropriate guidance where necessary, will they be accepted,' was the overall message.

Chapter 3

Pretoria

Having already spent time in the United Kingdom going through the National Directorate's whole-school evaluation policy and making, as I was expected to do, some recommendations for its improvement, I had been asked to return to South Africa to talk it through with members of the Quality Assurance Directorate. I had been booked into the Holiday Inn in Pretoria for a week in mid-April. It was reasonably close to the headquarters of the National Directorate for Quality Assurance which was the venue for the proposed meeting. The meeting was planned for my first day back in South Africa. I decided it would be a good idea to take Aurora to Pretoria with me, as there was to be a workshop at the end of the week in which the revisions I had suggested for the policy on whole-school evaluation were to be discussed. I foresaw the possibility of my needing Aurora's help at some stage during the workshop,

On our arrival, I again did as I had been advised to do by various people in South Africa and friends in England. In England, the message was, 'There are lots of dangers in South Africa. Be careful. You need to check if it's safe to go out and where it's safe to go.' The warning was still ringing in my ears as we booked into the hotel and the question had to be asked. 'We've just arrived in Pretoria and we'd like to have a walk down the High Street. Is it a problem?' The receptionist's response was, as it had been in Johannesburg, far from encouraging. 'If you go out, Sir, I suggest you stay within the vicinity of the hotel. You can just follow the road round the hotel. You'll be safe enough.' And that's what we did, my saying, 'We can't go further than this, everybody can see I'm an Englishman'.

Aurora's response was, 'Why should I worry? Everybody can see I'm Romanian.' We both laughed, but I reckon if we did have any problems nobody would take the trouble to differentiate between a white Englishman and a white Romanian. And so it was with some trepidation we walked the short distance around the hotel, passing several groups of people seemingly uninterested in us and making me wonder why we were getting so many warnings. We stuck to the advice we had been given, however, returning to the hotel after a very short walk, and then we retired to our room for the rest of the evening. Here we discussed the inevitable question, 'Why is there so much concern about where we walk?' without being able to resolve it.

The following morning I went as planned to meet with Todd and Dr Mgijima. The purpose of the meeting was to discuss the whole-school evaluation policy and the plans I had formulated for training those likely to be evaluating schools under the new system. Whilst I was with Todd and Dr Mgijima I had assumed Aurora would stay in the hotel or in our room for the day. It was when I returned to the hotel and our room to meet up with Aurora again and ask her how she had spent what must have been a boring day on her own, that she announced, with a look of satisfaction on her face, 'I was fine. Had a walk down Church Street. Fascinating.'

I was staggered. I could not believe she would do such a thing on her own, ignoring the warnings we had been given. All I could think of was the risk she had taken. 'What on earth made you do that?'

'Felt like a walk. I really enjoyed it. Saw lots of what looked like students standing around and wandered through a street market where I saw some very interesting things. Eventually, I reached a very impressive square. It had all the usual – statues, impressive buildings, plenty of people ...'

I couldn't believe what I was hearing. We had looked down Church Street on the previous evening and seen lots of people milling around and congregating in groups. I suspect it was no quieter on the following morning with its market and students. I was just beginning to sigh with relief at the fact that my wife had returned to the hotel safely when she said, 'Had a funny experience, though.'

'I'll bet,' I said, expecting her to say something about being approached by strangers.

'Went into a bookshop.' That made some sense, I thought, knowing Aurora was a graduate in literature and always keen to investigate what quality of books a bookshop was selling. 'It was all dark and shaded inside, sentimental music was playing, and then I realised I was in a sex shop. They had all sorts of sex toys and books on sex. I was outside in a flash.'

'I'm not surprised,' I said as we both laughed at the story. 'That'll teach you.'

'No, I felt perfectly safe and reckon it's not as bad as you think and everybody else is telling us. I don't see any problem with walking along the streets.'

I wasn't totally convinced but over the next few days we both became more and more adventurous in our evening walks. I went down Church Street with Aurora on my arm, jokingly asking if she wanted to pop into the darkened bookshop. We walked around the grand statue of former President Kruger, in top hat and frock coat, which stood in the centre of Church Square and the civic buildings which surrounded it, always conscious of what the receptionist had said. Nothing untoward happened, however, though our surprise at seeing a statue of Kruger and later in Cape Town a huge monument to Cecil Rhodes surrounded by lions, undisturbed and untouched now that the black South Africans had seen the end of apartheid and white supremacy was, to our minds, amazing. More so when we thought of what had happened to other leaders and their trappings in countries where there had been similar upheavals in Government, as, for example, in Romania, where the one-time leader Ceausescu and his wife had both been executed.

Our walks down Church Street suggested that perhaps our concerns about moving around Pretoria were unjustified. As a result, towards the end of our stay in Pretoria, we felt bold enough to walk along the street in the opposite direction. The road didn't have the stylish look of Church Street, and, as white people, we attracted looks from many of the black people standing chatting in groups at the entrances to the houses we passed. But nothing more. Our walk was not interrupted.

Thank goodness it wasn't, because it was along this road we discovered the impressive Union Buildings. This was the official seat of the South African Government and also where the National Department of Education was based along with several other Ministries, particularly those concerned with education. I had already learned that other Government offices were in the other two capital cities, Cape Town and Bloemfontein, places we were to visit later in the project.

I have never worked out which of the three cities is regarded as the most important, but Pretoria must figure high on the list. We knew, for instance, The Union Buildings, here in Pretoria, were those in which Nelson Mandela was inaugurated as President in 1994, an occasion which we had seen on television back home. We knew that it had been one of the greatest days in the recent history of South Africa and so we judged the Buildings would be well worth a visit.

We approached Union Buildings along a typical African city street. We were then 'gobsmacked' by what faced us. Superb terraced gardens, beautifully manicured, rose up to the impressive Union Buildings. They gave the committed gardener, Aurora, a good deal of pleasure as she came across many of South Africa's indigenous plants previously unknown to her, many of which would not grow in her native Romania or in England. As we moved up towards the centre of the Government buildings, built with their symmetrical towers and frontage, a style which appeared far more welcoming than Westminster, we passed a statue of South Africa's first Prime Minister, the horse-riding Louis Botha, and then a statue of the former President Hertzog, a great supporter of apartheid. He still stood proudly in the gardens, and to our surprise, like that of Kruger in Church Square, remained untouched. I've learned since it was taken down in 2013 and replaced by one of Nelson Mandela, a move which one would have expected to happen much earlier. We also passed the war memorial to those who died in the wars of the twentieth century.

Once we had reached the road which was in front of the Union Buildings we were able to walk along to view the impressive South African Police Memorial. We could also see in the distance the huge, imposing Voortrekker monument which remains in its usual position, high on a hill just south of Pretoria, unharmed, a memory of the Great Trek and a symbol of the Boers' desire for independence from the British and of the white South African's domination of their black and coloured countrymen.

It was on these walks we were tempted to think about going into restaurants but were dissuaded by being unsure as to whether we would be welcome in some of them. It was clear to us as we observed those who entered and left that some were used purely by the black and coloured citizens whilst others were used by whites. It was the same in some of the roadside bars, a fact I came across when travelling one day across country with Todd, and we stopped for a drink. He took me into a shebeen, where I attracted some attention by being the only white man in the place. But with Todd I was in safe hands and once the customers had become accustomed to my presence we all settled down to chatting and enjoying our drinks.

Aurora and I shared the opinion that we should be able to go into any restaurant – after all, I was working through the day with people from all the different cultures. However, the pressure got to us and we settled on going into a restaurant across from the hotel which appeared to have only white customers, though there was nothing, as far as we could see, which prevented black and coloured customers entering. It was here that Aurora celebrated her birthday by enjoying her most memorable tasting of a huge portion of pork ribs.

It was amazing how our confidence in moving about Pretoria grew from that very first foray of Aurora's and the cautious evening walks which followed. We began to feel comfortable moving around the main thoroughfares and came to know Pretoria quite well. I have to thank Aurora for that. Her venture down Church Street changed our approach to Pretoria and what it had to offer.

When we visited again in May we felt bold enough to walk down Church Street and along the side street which led us up to and beyond the Union Buildings. Amusingly, in doing so we became confused with some of the stragglers involved in a running road race. I was in shorts and t-shirt, enjoying the warm sun, without realising the message it was sending. As we passed a group of some kindly South Africans, I was given advice as to which route we should be taking. As usual, they warned against some streets, saying they could be dangerous and advised us to follow the white dots painted on the kerbside, which would, they said, lead us along the way towards our goal – the finish of the race.

I had no intention of going to the finish or even raising a jog, but we did continue our walk and did as advised by following the white dots. It is sad I need to record that there are still localities, even in Pretoria, as in all the large cities we visited, where we had to exercise great caution and avoid certain areas and streets.

Chapter 4

The National Conference

Once the policy on whole-school evaluation had been agreed with the Quality Assurance Directorate it had to be presented in a clearly written form which made the whole process of evaluation comprehensible to the government, the general public, the staff in schools and to the teachers' unions. My task when back in the UK was to continue to liaise with Todd and make recommendations as to the structure and wording of the policy in readiness for it being presented to the National Government for approval. In addition, I began to prepare a training programme based on the policy for those who were to become supervisors. I made a good deal of progress, both with the policy and the guidance on its implementation before I returned to South Africa later in May of the same year to finalise, in a workshop organised by the Directorate, the revised policy, the framework for its implementation, and what was to become the supervisors' handbook.

When I returned to South Africa at the end of the month the framework, guidance and criteria were finalised, helped by the fact that throughout my time in the United Kingdom I had remained in contact with Todd, seeking to ensure any suggestions I made were in line with the Directorate's intention.

The first significant task facing the Minister of Education, once the draft policy was agreed by the National Directorate, was to present it to interested parties and get their reaction before it was finalised and sent for ratification to the national government in Pretoria. The outcome was a two-day National Conference on whole-school evaluation in Caesar's Palace Conference Centre in Gauteng Province in September 2000, to which were invited over one hundred delegates from a wide range of interested parties, including the directors of the Provinces and representatives of the unions, universities, world bank and the national examination board. The Conference's purpose was to bring together representatives of interested parties to consider, through what was described as 'critical debate', the proposed policy, along with the criteria and guidelines for evaluation which had been agreed by the National Directorate. It was also designed to enable those with an interest in schools to consider international approaches to the supervision, quality assurance, monitoring and evaluation of the quality of education. A number of questions had been invited from the different groups before the Conference with the intention of ensuring that speakers and discussion groups focused on the main issues.

It was only the second time I had visited a casino. The first was in Romania when I went along with colleagues to use tickets we had been gifted by our travel agent for an evening meal and a couple of spins at the tables. Our visit didn't last long, especially as we gained nothing from the tables. My visit to Caesar's Palace lasted much longer, but not because of the gaming tables and slot machines. A swift walk through the area in which hopeful, blank faces stared at the spinning numbers on a machine, or a rotating ball at gaming tables controlled by scantily dressed, pretty young ladies brought me to the room in which the more sober educationists were gathering for the launch of the national policy on whole-school evaluation.

The Deputy Director General, Further Education and Training, Khetsi Lehoko of the Department of Education opened the proceedings, simply re-iterating the purpose of the conference which was, he said, 'another opportunity to discuss the (whole-school evaluation) policy framework and its implementation.' He went on to say he looked forward to the discussion, 'on some of the pertinent issues in the policy and how we can proceed collectively to raise standards in our schools.' I followed, reflecting on the difference between the new policy and the old style inspection associated with apartheid times, the importance of a school's internal self-evaluation and its likely impact on external whole-school evaluation, and emphasising the benefits to be gained from all schools being evaluated against agreed national criteria. If this could be achieved, I argued, strengths could be shared and improvements recommended which would have an impact nationally and, with Government support, help drive-up the overall quality of learning in the country's schools, no matter what type they were. I sought to dispel the fear that external evaluation meant external control, an outcome many South Africans believed had been the purpose of earlier systems of external inspections.

Questions raised as a result of what I had had to say concerned the impact it was likely to have on the provincial and national departments of education, which, technically, were responsible for schools. The questions reflected the concerns of many South Africans, who felt that the Provinces and National Government were not fulfilling their obligations, were somewhat ineffective and were continuing to treat the various types of school differently. The questioners wanted to know if their inadequacies would be exposed and whether or not the new policy would lead to a fairer distribution of resources across the whole of the education system.

Further questions were raised once the Conference had finished, with the teachers' unions, in particular, writing to Dr Mgijima. The National Professional Teachers' Organisation of South Africa (NAPTOSA), for example, sent in a detailed commentary in which it agreed that whole-school evaluation was probably the best way towards achieving quality in schools. But the union expressed some serious doubts as to whether the Government would have sufficient person power to implement the policy, that the training provided for supervisors may not overcome some of the fears held by schools and that the Government needed to ensure schools had sufficient resources as they endeavoured to move towards equality. The South African Teachers' Union (SAOU) expressed similar thoughts but added that attention should also be given to the Development

Appraisal System (DAS) aimed at improving the quality of teaching. This was a theme also taken up by The South African Democratic Teachers' Union (SADTU), which expressed further concerns about the availability of resources and the willingness of the different Provinces to support a national system.

Rand Afrikaans University also took the opportunity to comment on the national policy for whole-school evaluation, setting out five positive aspects of the policy, which included support for the policy's focus on school improvement, its emphasis on collaboration and its underlying principles of equity, equality and non-discrimination. The University's concerns related to the need for clear indicators of good practice, and more clarity as to the criteria used in appointing supervisors. .

On the other hand, the response of the Federation of Association of Governing Bodies of South African Schools (FEDSAS) was highly critical, seeing whole-school evaluation as another name for inspection and one which would intimidate rather than support schools.

A significant factor underlying concerns about how common the approach to raising school standards was, I learned in my discussions with Todd, was that the House of Representatives was the department which handled coloured children's schooling, the Department of Education and Training handled black children's schooling and the Education Ministry oversaw schools for white children, which were known as Model C Schools.

Not surprisingly, the questions rang bells for me. I had already had the privilege of visiting a few schools, and with Aurora had also observed village children on their way to school. Even in post-apartheid South Africa, there remained great discrepancies in the schools provided for different children, discrepancies which were easy to see but which were likely to take years to overcome. There is little doubt that the Education Minister faced a huge task in his efforts to implement Tirisano, not only in terms of his endeavour but also in terms of his finding sufficient resources to bring a measure of equality.

My impression was that the central government and the Provincial governments were keen to cater equally for all their children and this intention was in line with the strong desire for good education among the many black and coloured people with whom I spoke. The sight of young children from rural villages walking barefoot to a school which could be up to twelve miles distant, for example, their blouses and shirts crispy white and often with their shoes in their hands so that they remained presentable for school, were indicators of this desire which linger long in the mind. For both Aurora and me, they reflected the desire for education which the majority of South Africans clearly wanted for their children.

The inequalities which still existed became increasingly evident the more I visited South Africa. In one meeting, for instance, I came across representatives from independent schools, much the same as those in the United Kingdom, which catered for the wealthy and ambitious parents of white children. There were also delegates from the schools which had been termed 'Model C' schools, which, under apartheid, had been all white schools which had ten times more resources invested in them than the schools for black and coloured children. The Model 'C' school I visited had all the trappings of the schools I was used to visiting in England. Pupils were studying in clean and well-organised classrooms at appropriately sized desks; the buildings were in a good state of repair and were surrounded by grassed and hard-core play areas; and pupils had access to clean toilets and plenty of running water. In this 'Model C' school, the science laboratories were well equipped and had gas and electricity on tap. Throughout, the school was well decorated. As I had expected, the pupils were mostly white and smartly dressed in their school uniforms.

It was pleasing to note, however, in the post-apartheid period the Principal had made attempts to move with the changing times. Not only was he kind enough to welcome me into his school along with a black supervisor I was monitoring, he was also beginning to accept the basic principles of Tirisano and had, amongst the predominantly white pupils, the occasional black child. However, in keeping with a school of this type, all the teachers were white and trained and had at their disposal a wide range of resources such as overhead projectors and computers which contributed to their effectiveness. I didn't find it surprising that the school had some of the best examination results in the country.

In comparison, on the occasion Aurora and I were visiting friends in Hout Bay, I was told about what was described as a 'coloured school' at the far end of town. For those who do not know South Africa, Hout Bay is very much a white enclave about twenty miles outside Cape Town, which in many ways exudes wealth. It is described as 'The Republic of Hout Bay' by some of its citizens. I decided to pay an unannounced visit to the school, fascinated to learn what a 'coloured school' was and how it compared with the 'Model C' school. The head welcomed me and showed me round. As we visited different classrooms, it was clear the school was just for coloured children, taught by coloured teachers and led by a coloured headteacher. I found what I was seeing so different to my experiences in the 'Model C' school. I had been aware of the black versus white issues through the media back home and through my reading, but the emergence of another group, the coloureds, came as something of a surprise. It shouldn't have, because in many ways it was the natural outcome of the mix of populations.

The position of the coloureds in society was, I learned, even more ambiguous than that of the black citizens during the period of white supremacy, as they lacked not only the kudos of being white but neither were they black. As a result, they did not have the tribal connections which I found to be still so important in the new South Africa.

After my tour of the school I sat in the headteacher's office and discussed what I was doing in South Africa. He nodded, clearly hoping his school would benefit in some way from the proposed changes. He went on to outline the current problems he faced in some detail. He said he lacked sufficient teachers and so classes, as I had seen, were large and cramped into rooms too small; he had none of the technical appliances, such as overhead projectors, which would help learning; and he added that the range of text and exercise books was severely limited. He could see no solution until Tirisano was taken on board fully by the Provincial and National authorities. Only then, he said, would there be a chance of some equality in the educational system and a better deal for the children in his care. Unfortunately, like many South Africans I met, he had little concept of what it takes to make the sort of fundamental changes the country needed if educational provision was to have some parity for all children.

Whether or not the school was any better or worse than the one which I had visited in one of the shanty towns which catered only for black children, it is difficult to say. That school had been built in an open area on the edge of a township and the wood and concrete buildings were surrounded by what seemed like waste land. On that occasion, I had been staggered by what I found inside. The Principal proudly showed me a new science laboratory which had recently been opened, but which lacked access to gas or electricity and had no running water. In fact, the lack of mains water meant there were no toilets for the children and if they had a need, they were expected to go into the longer grass surrounding the school. I have to add, I never discovered what the staff were expected to do. The classrooms were overcrowded and the staff had nothing more than a small, well-used blackboard on which to write. Desks and chairs varied in size and quality and made it difficult for many of the children to concentrate on their studies.

Those visits made it even more obvious to me that the work I was involved in was critically important. It was obvious that much more would have to be done if the inequalities were to be overcome and the equalities spelled out in Tirisano were to be achieved.

But the differences in provision didn't end there and with those three types of school. My visit to what was described as a 'farm school' revealed further disparities in the opportunities offered to children. This was a school to which the children of many of the farm labourers went. Provided by the white farmers, generally at as little a cost as possible, such schools were seen, I was informed, as an ideal arrangement for the white farmers. When extra hands for the farm were required at particular times of the year I was told the farmer simply closed the school and made use of the pupils. In return, in the 'farm school' I visited, the farmer had provided a one classroom building in what looked more like a shack than a school. It served about twenty pupils, the children of the farm labourers, from across the age range.

The so-called school was very poorly equipped and depended on an unqualified teacher, who admitted she had difficulties ensuring pupils attended school regularly. Those who were present displayed little interest in the mundane teaching and when I spent some time talking to them found their English rudimentary. Most relied on their tribal language. They sat at desks not always of a suitable size whilst the teacher had to rely on a well-used blackboard, a lump of white chalk and a limited number of old, well-worn text books to support her efforts to educate the children. The possibility of there being a library in which the children could develop their reading skills was non-existent and there were no facilities for physical activities other than the open fields and a few trees outside the building, which also served as the children's toilets.

I knew nothing of the overall economic position of South Africa, but after visiting the different types of school it was obvious that there were great differences in the financial support they were given and that systems which had been used to seek to improve the quality of education for all children since 1984 and the Education Act of 1996 were not yet working as effectively as had been hoped. The desire of the National Directorate to find a system for evaluating all schools against common criteria and so allow them to be able to demonstrate to the Ministry how many pupils were still suffering because of the inequality became even clearer than it had been when I first arrived in South Africa.

And yet, whatever efforts we were likely to make, it was difficult to see how whole-school evaluation of itself would be sufficient to rid South Africa of the discrepancies. The system of whole-school evaluation, if implemented properly, might enable those keen to bring equality to speak with more authority about the difficulties being faced in many schools, but unless the system ensured clear messages were brought to the attention of the National Government about the 'why's' and the 'wherefore's' which were resulting in the differences, it was unlikely that much would be done to right the issues. The teachers' unions and those who raised such issues at the National Conference had a point!

However, the immediate solution of the unions, investment in teacher appraisal and staff development, although beneficial to schools, was also unlikely to overcome the problems at the speed required by Tirisano or of Nelson Mandela.

It was this which convinced me that the drawing together of different evaluation reports on schools from the different Provinces into a national report for the Minister of Education was going to be essential. I had already discussed the possibility of this with the National Directorate, but once I had more evidence of how slowly things were changing I raised the idea again and it was willingly accepted. The recommendation was helped by the presence of a speaker from the Office for Standards in Education in England, Mark Griffiths, (Chief Inspector, Further Education Funding Council), at the National Conference in September 2000. The fact that he was invited to speak about experiences in England indicated how much the South African Ministry wanted to share ideas on practice and outcomes with other countries. This desire became an important factor which helped in preparing the way for the putting together of an annual national report in which the evaluation findings from different Provinces could be communicated to the Ministry as an overview of what was happening in education throughout South Africa.

The discussions with the National Directorate revealed there were 29,000 schools of one type or another in South Africa. I sought to demonstrate to the National Directorate that it would take something like 1000 trained supervisors, operating in very small teams and working as full-time supervisors, three and a half years to evaluate them; that is if they were to have the time to evaluate them effectively. Compared to the desire of the Ministry, which was looking for a country-wide evaluation within the year, the longer time frame was a more likely target, I argued, and, with sufficient resources in terms of trained supervisors, one possible to meet.

The solution devised by the National Directorate was to train as many supervisors as possible in all nine Provinces so that as many schools as possible could be evaluated. They believed the information could then be drawn into a single report to be presented to the Minister. It all added up to extending my task from helping to draw up an evaluation policy and training a number of supervisors to carry out evaluations, to one which meant training more supervisors in every Province and more quickly than had first been envisaged. It also implied the need to train the best of these to become what were to be known as facilitators, that is supervisors able to train other supervisors, and also draw up a national report for the Minister based on any whole-school evaluations carried out in the different Provinces. I had become so involved in the project and so keen to help South Africa achieve its goal of improving the overall quality of education, that I willingly agreed to do as asked. Consequently, the plan was put into action during October and November of 2000 when I visited several different Provinces and managed to train over two hundred supervisors and facilitators.

Chapter 5

The Drakensburg Mountains

The course for supervisors in the Gauteng Province was held in Boxburg, a suburb of Johannesburg. Having been introduced to the thirty or so course members, black, coloured and white by Todd, I sought, as usual, to ease the tension for me, if not for the trainees, with a joke.

'I would be surprised,' I said, 'if, as supervisors, you didn't find children to be your greatest allies in school when evaluating. A simple question, 'Is there anything different this week?' can sometimes get the response, 'Well, yes. Our teacher's been in every day.' I knew it would amuse, because it was well known attendance by teachers could be erratic and present the sort of problem which the Ministry was trying to overcome. And then, 'I watched a young pupil putting different articles into a bowl of water. 'What are you doing?' I asked.

'Seeing what floats and what doesn't.'

'And what have you found out?'

'That big things sink and little things float.'

'I couldn't resist the temptation. I picked up a large piece of wood and a very small ball bearing and put them in the water. The wood floated and the small ball bearing sank. 'And what d'you make of that?'

'The child looked at me, eyes wide and rubbing her chest. She said 'I'm wearing a new vest today.' The joke raised a laugh from the trainees but for once I managed to avoid the '…Oh…kay…' response.

When the trainees had settled I proceeded, in this first session, to outline the new policy for school evaluation. Aurora had joined me in South Africa and at the end of the first session she helped to prepare the conference room for the next session which was group work. I had set course members various group tasks and Aurora used the break between sessions to place the appropriate papers on the trainees' work tables in readiness.

One of the tasks was concerned with stressing the importance of studying a school's documentation and talking to the headteacher in order to learn as much about the school as possible before the actual external evaluation began. I had collected some documentation from English schools and so, once I had made them anonymous, I was able to provide brief samples of what the supervisors would hope to find in the schools they were to evaluate. In the main, the session went well, especially when the teasing about my Yorkshire accent began again, and in particular when I used the words 'budget' and 'bundle', whilst the black South Africans could not avoid using the word 'Oh…kay…', when I asked them to settle to their work. There is no doubt that we established what I took to be a very good relationship.

It wasn't long, however, before the task brought a response from course members I had not anticipated. My question before they began the task, 'Are there any questions?' produced comments which I hadn't expected but which, as I sought to answer them, I knew I should have foreseen. They were comments for which my experience in visiting schools in South Africa should have prepared me. 'Many schools don't have documentation;' 'Most teachers don't do lesson plans;' and, 'Few subjects have written policies.' One comment brought nods all around the room. 'Some schools wouldn't have enough paper to do any of this, anyway.' Then followed the obvious question, 'So what do we do?' I could only answer, 'You take what they've got.'

The frustration among the course members was obvious and so I went on, 'But you need to help them see the value in having such documentation, both for an internal and an external evaluation. You should now be able to give them some idea of what documents would be helpful to them in delivering a worthwhile educational experience to their pupils, and then suggest ways in which they might go through the process of writing them, even if it's only basic. You should also report the shortages and hope the district officials will do something about it.'

The suggestion led to further discussion about the problems schools might have and how they would impact on what the supervisors could expect from them. And then, of course, 'What are we to do if there is no documentation?' I offered some suggestions, the most obvious being the need to talk with the principal, as headteachers were invariably known as in South Africa, and with other members of staff who may have relevant information. I emphasised that the conversations had to be carefully recorded in their own notebook so that the evidence could be contained in the evaluation report. 'It is only if you have written evidence that there is any chance the District officers will take any notice,' I added. Trainees looked at one another and began to mumble something which I interpreted as their saying, 'Some hope,' but eventually I managed to get them settled to discuss the tasks I had given them. I hoped the exercise would encourage them to look for this sort of evidence when they evaluated schools and provide an insight into its value. There is no doubt the exercise stimulated discussion and some useful responses before I brought the session to a close with a plenary. Subsequent sessions throughout the week concerned contact with the school and the Principal, planning an evaluation for the team of supervisors, the use of the different evaluation forms, the evaluation of educational provision, the conduct of team meetings, the eventual feedback to the Principal and staff, and the writing of the report.

At midday on the first day I joined the course members and Todd in the hotel's restaurant for lunch. For really the first time I began to hear the different languages as friends grouped together around the tables. I had no idea what was being said or what the languages were, but sat with what, at times, must have been a perplexed look on my face. I could only guess that some would be using Koi Koi, some would be speaking in Xchosa, some in Twasana and others in Sotho. It was possible all the eleven official languages of South Africa may have come into play – certainly English did when I wanted to speak. It was not only the different languages which surprised me. I was also struck by the amount of meat the South Africans had on their plates, a very common habit I learned through experience, but the reason for which I had to guess as it was never explained to me.

Perplexed I may have been, but it would be wrong to say I was ignored. When those around me reverted to English I picked up a good deal of information about attitudes to the new government, the issues surrounding education, and the significance of tribal connections. The last of these was, I gathered, to become an issue for Todd when he discovered he had a new secretary who was from a different tribe to his own. He had not been consulted about the appointment and made it known he was not pleased about it. As far as I could see, he was simply reflecting the strong tribal ties which still existed in the country.

During lunch I also learned of what was described as, 'An excellent place to spend a weekend.' Aurora and I had planned to spend a few more days in South Africa after the course had finished, once more hoping to have the opportunity to gain more knowledge of a country with which we were greatly impressed. When I asked the question, 'Where d'you think we could spend a few days not too far away?' the general response was the Drakensbergs. With a little more probing I learned of a hotel called 'Little Switzerland.' I was fascinated by the name, thinking, *'How does Little Switzerland end up in South Africa?'* I had no immediate answer to that question and I didn't bother to enquire further about the name – there are plenty of hotels and restaurants in the United Kingdom which bear names which seem to be out of place. For instance, 'L'escargot bleue' may or may not have something to do with blue snails, or even France. Having decided to follow advice and book a weekend at the hotel, Aurora and I were to learn why it had been recommended.

When the course had finished we headed for the Drakensbergs and Little Switzerland. We discovered a delightful place. We were so impressed that we agreed that sometime in the future we would return to have a proper holiday and enjoy the delights, not only of the hotel but of the area around. Journeys around the Drakensbergs, I guessed, would provide a wonderful holiday.

I was right. On our next visit to *Little Switzerland* we stayed long enough to enjoy all that the Drakensbergs had to offer. The hotel was overlooked by the mountains and provided a fantastic view of what we came to know as the amphitheatre of the Drakensbergs. The outlook from our room at the rear of the hotel engaged us each time we returned to it, whether it was from the excellently presented meal in the restaurant, a walk on the paths which surrounded the hotel, or from a trip to one of the well known sites within driving distance.

Immediately in front of our room were two gazebo, which tempted us out on more than one occasion to drink coffee under their thatched roofs; just beyond them was a kraal in which several horses twisted and turned as they looked for the best feeding area, sometimes being willing to contest for the space; and then, beyond, was the valley, which stretched way into the distance.

We had reached the hotel by driving from Johannesburg and joining the main N3 road which took us towards the quiet town of Harrismith, a town noted for being, at one-time, very much a white settlement. We left the main road and went into the town, first to get a sight of its streets and buildings but also to see whether it had a Catholic church. It was this town, we reckoned, which would be the nearest one in which we could attend Mass on the Sunday. I mention this for no particular reason, other than to record the unusual circumstances surrounding the Sunday Mass we attended.

On the Sunday morning we arrived at the church in good time, along with others, but as the minutes passed and the priest didn't arrive on the altar, we began to fear that for some inexplicable reason there would be no Mass that day. It was some fifteen minutes after the Mass should have started and the hymn singing was beginning to flag before one of the parishioners, seemingly versed in such matters, decided to lead a non-sacramental service from the lectern on the altar. He was part-way through what for us was an unusual experience when another parishioner approached him and whispered in his ear. To everyone's delight, he was able to announce that the priest had arrived.

The priest began Mass with an apology, saying he had had to travel a good distance to get to the church, and then proceeded to celebrate Mass. I suspect we were not the only ones in church who began to worry when the Mass took an unusual course. The priest carried on confidently even when he completely omitted the consecration of the bread and wine, the essential element of the Mass. It was only after we had started to say the closing prayers that he stopped, a shocked look on his face, with, 'I'm very sorry. I've forgotten the consecration.' He returned back behind the altar to do what he should have done minutes before, consecrate the bread and wine. To say that the whole congregation was staggered is to underestimate the rumble of disgruntlement which Aurora and I could sense. I could imagine the thoughts going through the minds of the white congregation at the mistake made by the black priest. But the error had to be accepted and everyone kneeled to allow the priest to go through what he should have done much earlier in the Mass. After all, he was a priest, had been blessed with sacramental powers and was the only one in the church who could consecrate the bread and wine. At the appropriate time, those of us in the congregation who wished to receive communion processed up to the altar as usual to receive the Body and Blood of Christ. It seemed the mistake had been forgotten. Having returned to our places to continue with our prayers, we were blessed by the priest and departed from the strangest Mass we had ever attended.

After Mass we left Harrismith and headed back to our hotel, still trying to understand what had happened in church, but recognising how fortunate we had been in finding such a beautiful hotel in which to spend a few days. It was a hotel which offered a good deal within its doors and within its immediate neighbourhood, but more than that, we quickly recognised that among the most appealing features of Little Switzerland was its position. Not only did it provide a super view of the Drakensbergs but it also had within easy striking distance two famous landmarks of the Boer War, both of which I had heard of in history lessons at school. In addition, close by was probably the highest waterfall in the world, the Tugela Falls, which we were to see as we travelled through the mountainous countryside.

As for the Boer War, one site we felt worthy of a visit was the city of Ladysmith, the scene of a significant siege in 1899. It was here that British troops were hemmed in by the Boer army and only the arrival of a much larger British force some months later relieved the town and provided the food and water the inhabitants desperately needed. The siege of Ladysmith had been an event in the Boer War which had stuck in my mind since the age of fifteen and there I was, by chance, standing within its historic streets.

Along the high street we passed the great gun shops, the Dutch reformed church, the impressive Soofi Mosque, with its tall white turrets, and the war museum. We didn't go into the museum because time was pressing and we had another major highlight in the surrounding mountains which I, in particular, was desperate to visit. We were both impressed by the architecture of the town and the sense of space and the beauty of the area within which it was set, recurring themes as we travelled to different places in South Africa.

Eventually, we climbed Gordon's Hill where the main war memorials dedicated to the British and Boer armies stood, though they were not the only memorials we saw. Different regiments had placed, in different parts of the town, their recognition of what the troops had suffered. They were clear reminders of those harsh days of struggle for supremacy between the British and the Boers at the end of the nineteenth century and the beginning of the twentieth.

Once we were back in the car I drove to our next destination to see what it could tell us about South Africa's past. Sadly, it told us a great deal more about the horrors of war. Our destination was the Spion Kop. I knew of the battle which had occurred, the bravery displayed by both sides, the tragic mistakes made by officers and the desperate loss of life, but to visit and see such a place which had been bequeathed by history to observers like Aurora and me was both shocking and inspiring. The line of graves of the British soldiers, all of them named and many of them under twenty years of age, bordered by white stone and headed by a white cross, followed the line of trenches in which they died. But it was difficult not to feel sorry for those Boers who had also died there.

We had seen the memorials to Boers and British in Ladysmith, but their impact seemed to diminish as I stood on one of the most famous battlefields I had heard about in my school history. I couldn't help wonder how many of their relatives and friends had been able to do more than grieve, unable to afford to come to South Africa to visit the graves and pay their respects in the traditional manner, and then I thought of the many Kops in England in football and rugby grounds, the most famous being Anfield and its Spion Kop. In their own way they were memorials to these young men who had fought for their Queen and country, though the journalist who first coined the name had probably never visited South Africa.

For Aurora, the impact of standing on Spion Kop was not the same as it was for me. Although she felt sorrow for those who had died she knew nothing of the Boer War other than what we had learned in the few days we were staying in Little Switzerland, and she found it difficult to empathise with those she saw simply as colonialists – 'People prepared to risk the lives of others for their own gain,' as she put it. She could only wonder why so many lives had been lost to support a class system which she could not understand, one which had been wiped clean in her own country as a result of the principles under which the communists ruled.

What was drawing us to battlefields I wasn't sure, but we also decided to visit Blood River. It was here, I knew again from my history lessons, that in 1838 the Voortrekkers, Boers on the Great Trek from Western Cape and the British laws which were being introduced there, had a memorable battle with the Zulu. I knew the outline of the story from my school history. It was here that a small number of Voortrekkers defeated a very much larger force of Zulu, killing many and causing the river to flow with Zulu blood, hence its name. The Voortrekkers had succeeded by creating a ring of wagons, a laager, behind which they were well protected and from behind which they could fire at the charging enemy, who gained little protection from their spears and shields. I imagined the defensive position taken by the Voortrekkers was much the same as I had seen on films of the Wild West, when settlers moving across America were attacked by Indians. The films portrayed exciting gunfire, arrows striking unfortunate settlers, the formation of the wagons into a circle as the settlers sought to create fortress-like defences, and the Indians being repulsed. The startlingly real laager which we saw at what was now known as Blood River brought back the memories. The metal wagons which have been circled to replicate the situation in 1838 leave little to the imagination, especially when seen in the context of information displayed in the nearby Voortrekker museum and passed on by the museum's curator.

Across the river is the Zulu museum. We were shown round by a young Zulu student whose response to the question, 'How did you learn so much about the Battle of Blood River?' was simply, 'Quality time with my grandma.' The way he said it reminded me of the way many black children learned about their history and the problems likely to be faced as efforts were made to produce the history text books required by schools. What history would they contain?

The student was enthusiastic about what he was telling us, immersed in the bravery of his tribe, a quality which history has portrayed as a key characteristic of the Zulu, and we couldn't help but be stirred by the pride he showed in his forefathers, even though they had suffered a terrible defeat. Our eagerness to learn what we could of how the Zulu interpreted those events and to what extent it modified what I had been taught left us with little time to move on to our next destination.

As a result, when we arrived at Rourke's Drift, the museum was already closed for the day and we had no opportunity to see it or get a guided tour of the nearby location of another famous battle, Islandwana. The curator did, however, point out the fields which were overlooked by our position at Rourke's Drift, fields on which it is said the British suffered one of their worst defeats in South Africa and where a large part of the British force was massacred. At Islandwana, the Zulu success against better armed troops sent an unpalatable message back to the government in Westminster. But as luck would have it, a more insignificant battle occurred later that day when the Zulu leading a force of warriors disobeyed his chief and attacked Rourke's Drift. His foolhardiness led to defeat for the Zulus and victory for the British, who risked everything to save the hospital and the lives of those in it. To avoid the castigation of the British public, the government ensured that the success at Rourke's Drift and the number of Victoria Crosses which were awarded for bravery in that particular encounter, though clearly deserved, received much higher publicity than the defeat at Islandwana.

We managed to get lost on our way back to Little Switzerland and the dipping evening sun, which had cast a shadow over the battlefield earlier, became our guide. Warned as we had been on so many occasions about the dangers when travelling off the main thoroughfares, especially at night, our nerves were on edge as we travelled along the seemingly endless country roads. We found some comfort in the fact that the doors and windows of the hire car automatically locked once the engine was switched on, but we couldn't help but have our blood racing each time we passed a group of Africans, though we never had the need to suspect any danger. Their surprised stares seemed full of wonderment at seeing a car containing white people in areas they regarded as their own.

Despite our anxiety, and before it became too dark, we took pleasure in being able to have a view of Zulu villages and gain a sense of Zulu life. We looked with interest at the mix of tin shacks and well-constructed straw-covered huts, groups standing by water pumps, women rather than men carrying the buckets balanced on their heads, the bareness which typified the villages and the apparent absence of livestock. We also wondered what access they had to the basic facilities such as readily available lighting, an amenity which is taken for granted in many other areas of the world. However, they were a far cry from the cluttered, ill-kept townships which we had seen around the main towns we had passed through.

Gradually, as the sun faded, our concerns grew again, but when I look back on the journey and the time we spent in South Africa, I wonder why. I never really felt threatened, and although Aurora was to have an unpleasant experience in Durban, she, too, felt no less safe than she did in her native land. Having said we never really felt threatened, it was with a good deal of relief that we eventually reached the main road and were able to make our way back to the hotel.

When we reached the hotel we were able to enjoy an excellent meal served by a black waiter who knew more about English football than I did. It was only when he raised questions about Leeds United that I came into my own and was able to talk with some authority about the great days of Revie, Bremner, Giles and Lorimer. The conversation continued the following morning with our exchanging views on teams such as Manchester United, Arsenal and Liverpool.

Aurora and I then set off on another day of exploration. On this occasion we headed for Clarens, a town situated to the North East of the hotel, with the intention of spending some time walking and exploring the countryside. When we reached the town, about which we had heard a good deal, we could not help but be impressed. The town and the mountains which surrounded it were captivating. Having parked the car we wandered along streets bordered with trees, well cared for gardens and high quality houses.

Eventually, we headed along a country path in the direction of more hilly country. Our intention was to gain a wider and hopefully more exciting view of the town and its surrounding area. Suddenly, we came to a halt. In the soft dust of the path were the marks of a huge paw. I looked around, a tingle creeping into the back of my neck. 'What d'you reckon, Aurora?' We both looked ahead to see whether the imprint continued up the hill or perhaps to see whatever animal had left it behind. Aurora replied, as she looked even closer at the print, 'It's definitely not the sort of cat's paw you see in England. I think we go back.' I couldn't have agreed more. 'No question of it,' I said and we turned and headed back along the path towards the car far quicker than we had walked away from it , knowing that there were other beauties in the Drakensberg Mountains for us to enjoy.

As we turned back to Clarens, always wary of what might be behind us, we took out our tour guide and began to identify in the distance sights such as Cathedral Peak, Champagne Castle and Giants' Castle, all of which overlooked the small town and wondered if they were worth a visit. But I had little time to find out. I had a course to run from the beginning of the following week.

Chapter 6

Mount Grace

The plan to train new supervisors in each of the nine Provinces was, as I have indicated earlier, put into effect after the Minister's Conference in Gauteng in September 2000, which had been held to launch the national policy on whole-school evaluation. The intention, a sensible one, was to seek to ensure common practice in school evaluation throughout the country and in doing so put the Quality Assurance Directorate in a position to advise the Minister on what was required if the 'equality for all' principles underlying Tirisano were to be implemented. It meant my travelling to several Provinces towards the end of 2000 and returning to South Africa early in the following year to continue to carry out the training of the new supervisors and also a new group who were to be called facilitators.

The role of this new group emerged from my discussions with Todd and Dr Mgijima, in which we agreed it was necessary to create a group of people capable of both training new supervisors and of monitoring the evaluation process. We believed that if we could create a well-trained group, specialists in monitoring and reporting on the quality of school evaluations, we would be taking a significant step in ensuring the new policy was being implemented consistently across the country. We also felt that by creating such a group we would be laying foundations for the future development of the evaluation system once my consultancy had come to an end and I had returned to England. However, as I had learned, much depended on the authorities in individual Provinces as to whether whole-school evaluation was to be fully adopted. There was still a good deal of work to be done to convince some officials of the benefits of working within a nationally coordinated system. For example, it took Western Cape Province over a year before deciding to request training for its supervisors because it took the Province that long to finally decide to adopt the new policy. I gathered from different conversations that the hesitation may have been related to political differences rather than educational ones, because when they came on stream at the end of the following year the local education leaders and district officials entered with great enthusiasm.

Keen to make sure the policy was workable and acceptable, in January, 2001, the National Directorate decided to test out the new system of evaluating schools by carrying out what it termed 'pilot evaluations'. Early in February I carried out further training with the pilot strongly influencing what I did, and over several days I trained a core group, the facilitators, in readiness for monitoring these pilot evaluations. In addition, I spent time with the supervisors appointed to lead the evaluations in seven of the country's nine Provinces. I agreed with Todd it would make sense for me to have some oversight of the monitoring and of the application of the whole-school evaluation policy. This would help me judge whether or not the facilitators were well enough trained for their role and also to check on the effectiveness of the supervisors. It meant my travelling to seven of the nine Provinces: Northern Province and the Provinces of Kwa-Zulu Natal, Gauteng, Mpumlanga, Northern Cape, Free State and Eastern Cape. My travels ensured I was getting to know South Africa pretty well. I could have written a pretty boring story about its airports and the time I spent in them. I remember on one occasion, for instance, having missed an earlier flight, spending a lonely couple of hours or so in Kimberley airport awaiting a connection to Johannesburg.

By early March, 2001, Todd was able to issue a bulletin in which he reported that the first stage of the national monitoring of the pilot evaluations had been completed and in which he also summarised the outcome of the evaluations. The pilot had been carried out in the seven Provinces named above and in twelve schools. All the visits had been monitored by the newly trained specialist facilitators. The bulletin was upbeat, but I suppose one would expect it to be. The National Directorate had invested a good deal of time and effort in the project and I have no doubt their superiors at the Ministry were watching the outcome with special interest.

Later that month, Todd issued a more detailed report based on further school visits in the seven Provinces. In some Provinces up to six schools had been evaluated in line with the new policy. The evaluations provided the National Directorate and me with some important and useful information. They indicated that whole-school evaluation was acceptable to the principals and staff in the schools which had been part of the pilots, and their responses suggested it would also be acceptable to their colleagues in other schools.

The pilots also demonstrated that the supervisors had been sufficiently trained and skilled to carry out what were accepted as credible evaluations in the different types of school which they had visited. In addition, there was a general feeling that the advice given by supervisors and the subsequent improvement plans, based on their findings and produced by the school, could help schools improve their ability to self-evaluate and, more significantly, help to improve educational provision. Another positive aspect was the willingness with which most of the schools had been prepared to release teachers who had been trained as supervisors to carry out the evaluations. A further encouraging sign was the willingness of most of the Provincial authorities to support the project by providing what resources and equipment they could for the supervisors.

As I expected, however, the pilots revealed some classic defects – I had not spent almost twenty years inspecting schools in England without coming across them. Facilitators reported that supervisors' grades did not always match the text on the observation forms they were expected to complete; occasionally, the pre-evaluation process of reading and recording what little documentation there was in most of the schools visited had not been carried out thoroughly enough; that several schools didn't have any written documentation and the supervisors, therefore, were ill-prepared for their visit; and team leaders did not always record what other supervisors had done. This was especially the case in relation to which classes had been observed. Another common failing was the poor quality of some of the written reports. This was a weakness which Todd highlighted for further training, because without it the reports would not provide the accurate or detailed records required by the Provincial and National authorities or by the schools.

There were other factors identified which no amount of training would be likely to resolve. Something I learned as a result of the pilot and could see as a stumbling block was the fact that the supervisors were also teachers and, in order to protect their own professional jobs and their salaries, had to gain permission from their principals to be released so they could carry out the evaluations. It was a practice I had come across in Romania where I had advised that inspectors tied to their teaching jobs would never be able to create the sort of professional body required to ensure consistency and validity across the country. I gave similar advice to the National Directorate but it was clear they didn't really have the power to change the system.

As a result, we had a plus in that the supervisors continued to have hands-on experience in the classroom, but a possible minus in that the supervisors would have to seek release from their schools if they were to be involved in any external evaluations. This dual role meant they would also need regular training if there was to be consistency in the way they conducted whole-school evaluations and in the way they reported their findings.

A further issue was that the positive approach adopted by some of the Provinces was not taken on board by all. It came to light that two of the Provinces involved in the pilot had failed to provide their supervisors with either the transport or the equipment they needed to enable them to carry out the evaluations. Their reason – *'We don't have enough resources to carry out all the other responsibilities we have.'* As a result, some supervisors could not arrive at the school on the pre-arranged date and all the preparations made for the evaluation went to waste. Inevitably, the schools and the supervisors in these Provinces were frustrated and expressed their distrust of the whole process, believing the system would never work.

These concerns, which Todd included in his report, were not going to be resolved merely through arranging further training – it was going to need recognition at the highest level that, unless the support supervisors required was provided by the Provinces and their districts, no amount of training would produce the desired outcomes in educational provision.

Todd's helpful report led to my having to give further thought to the framework for training. I now recognised the training had to ensure Provincial and district officers, as well as supervisors, fully understood their roles and realised what it meant for them to give the system their full support. They were not to see themselves, on one hand, as distant officials with limited responsibility for the whole range of schools in their care, or simply as supports for external evaluators in the old apartheid style, willing to treat school principals and staff with disrespect. It was important that future training stressed the importance of the role of the districts in avoiding the mistreatment of schools, because, if that happened, schools would go back to resenting what they would come to consider the old style, unwarranted, external interference. There would then be only one outcome. The status of the new policy would be severely undermined and attitudes would revert to pre-1994. When I expressed such reservations to Todd and Dr Mgijima they agreed and encouraged me to look again at the training framework.

Despite having recognised the above difficulties, it is fair to say the National Directorate and I were, overall, pleased with how well the pilot evaluations had gone and how well the new facilitators had done their job. As monitors of the new system, they had submitted some useful conclusions. They reported the majority of supervisors approached their work conscientiously, created good relations with principals and ran well organised meetings with their co-supervisors. Most facilitators' reports recorded that the supervisors had provided effective oral feedback to the schools; they had complimented them on their strengths and carefully reported on any weaknesses they had discovered. In addition, they gave good advice where they could on what the school might do to overcome any of the areas of concern and in doing so improve the quality of educational provision.

The facilitators also reported that the majority of principals and staff responded positively to whole-school evaluation and to the way it was conducted. According to the reports, a number of the principals had said they saw the techniques used as being part of a process which would help them carry out another aspect of the Ministry's policy, effective internal evaluations of their own schools.

These were things I had hoped to hear and further enthused my approach to training. But when I had further time to study the reports I found the pilot had, as I mentioned earlier, revealed critical defects which could well undermine the approach to whole-school evaluation. The most serious of these was the lack of adequate resources for the process of external evaluation.

This issue became a reality for me on the occasion I went to monitor one of the pilot evaluations. When I arrived at the district office I was told the only car available to the supervisors and the district office had already been taken out. As a result, it would not be possible to transport me to the school I was supposed to visit. It was a situation I found difficult to comprehend but one which I had learned from the report was not uncommon. I was left wondering how, with such limited resources, any national system could be supported. I saw it as imperative that the Ministry should be alerted to the problems and so I put together a table of significant organisational issues raised by the pilot. It included the need for more permanent contracts for supervisors and facilitators if a regular system of evaluation were to be introduced; the need for a body to retrieve information from reports nationally so that the Government and the Provinces could be kept abreast of the needs of Provincial districts and schools; the strengthening and better resourcing of district staff to ensure facilitators, supervisors and schools had appropriate support; and the continuous training of supervisors to ensure they improved their skills in making qualitative judgements and writing effective reports.

These were critical issues and ones which existed at the different levels in the education system. I, and those in the National Directorate, believed they needed to be resolved if whole-school evaluation was to have the effect it was designed to achieve. We couldn't help but be concerned.

I found an opportunity to reflect on the findings of the pilot reports a few days after I had read it. The advantage of having Aurora with me on many of my visits to South Africa meant I could, on occasions, find opportunities between professional commitments to relax, think and review. But just as importantly, it gave both of us opportunities to visit places which neither of us would otherwise ever have seen. From our base in Pretoria, for example, we were able to spend the weekend between my commitments on this particular visit in what was a highly recommended 'getaway', Mount Grace.

I hired a car and still trying to think through solutions to the problems raised by the pilot evaluations drove a few miles beyond Johannesburg to Mount Grace. It was a hotel which was set in beautiful grounds. It had all the amenities enjoyed, we guessed, by many white people in the days before 1994. The only black people we saw even then, in 2001, while we were on that weekend jaunt, were cleaning and serving. But we could not be other than impressed by their efforts and what they were helping to provide.

The calm which surrounded Mount Grace gave me an opportunity to think through how I needed to approach future training if some of the critical issues were to be addressed, and what messages I needed to share with the National Directorate so as to help Todd and Dr Mgjima. The fact that Aurora and I had to do little more than sun ourselves in front of the small thatched cottage in which we were lodged for the weekend provided the ideal opportunity.

There is no doubt that my thoughts were stimulated by what we also enjoyed on that weekend. Our immediate view from the cottage was of a small pond covered with water lilies, and beyond was a panorama which seemed to stretch for ever as we viewed it from high up on the Magaliesberg Mountains on which the hotel was situated. We took the opportunity to relax, discuss our thoughts on what life must have been like for some in the days of apartheid, and prepare a response to the findings of the pilot. To be white in the days of apartheid must have been, as Aurora said with a touch of sarcasm, 'Very romantic.' It was a statement which veiled the plight of the majority of South Africans, but which probably summed up the experiences of some of their white countrymen.

I have to admit, we had a wonderful weekend. But time remained pressing and I had to collect my thoughts for the week ahead. We had just completed a hard two to three weeks in which a good number of new supervisors had been trained and during which I had learned the need to modify once more the framework for the training. I had to do this under some pressure as on our return to Pretoria we faced the start of another week of training. Fortunately, the weekend had provided an opportunity, not only for relaxation, but for me to identify the areas of training which required emphasis if the impact of whole-school evaluation was to be in line with the requirements of the National Directorate.

The preparations for our return to Pretoria went as expected. We loaded our belongings, paid our bill and climbed into the car. The first pull on the starter produced nothing more than a gasp. The second pull produced even less and by the time I had tried the starter several times I realised the car was not going to respond to my efforts. Aurora looked on anxiously. It was mid-afternoon. For once, we had accepted the advice to be back at the hotel in Pretoria before dark, and so we had decided to set off at a reasonable time. The last thing we needed was a problem with the car.

'Damned thing won't start,' I said with a frustrated look.

'What are we going to do? You've to be back in Pretoria for the course which starts tomorrow.'

'Don't you think I know it?' I couldn't help but sound a little vexed at Aurora saying the obvious but then we both went quiet as we tried to think through a solution. 'I'll have to go into the hotel and ask if they can find the telephone number of the hire firm. I'll have to ring them.'

'What then?' Aurora asked.

'I don't know. They have some sort of responsibility for us.' Asking myself how much responsibility and how such a wonderful weekend could come to such a sad end, I went into the hotel and asked if the receptionist could find the hire firm's number. We were in luck. She found it and she put me through. I went back outside to tell Aurora that help should arrive in about an hour's time. In the meantime, we could do no more than wait and exchange views on how we were likely to get back to Pretoria. We agreed the pair of us may arrive at our hotel sitting behind John, that was the name I had been given of the chap who would be coming out to help us, as he drove us back to Pretoria; we also discussed the possibility of my being at the wheel of the car as it was towed back to base; our third solution was to see the car on the back of a lorry whilst we were sitting in the cab with the driver; and our fourth was to think it possible for the car to be repaired and my driving it back to the hotel in Pretoria. The last option was beginning to cause concern for both of us as we saw the lights come on in and around the hotel and darkness creeping in. *'How will we find our way if it's dark by the time we reach Pretoria?'* I began to wonder.

More anxieties began to rumble through my mind as I sat with Aurora in the hotel lounge awaiting John. It took longer than the expected hour for him to make his way from Pretoria to Mount Grace. When he arrived, he cheerfully asked, 'What's the problem?' and didn't look at all phased by my answer, 'The damned thing won't start.'

'Let's have a look,' he said, in no way embarrassed about the situation we found ourselves in because of a car he had personally handed over to us. He lifted up the car bonnet and fiddled. 'Try starting it again.' I did but with no more success than I had had earlier. His head went under the bonnet and he fiddled again. 'Try it,' he called. This time, the car sparked into life. I uttered a sigh of relief, which was matched by Aurora's, 'Thank God.'

John came round to the door of the car, asked me to switch off and start again. Everything went smoothly. 'You'll be alright now. I'll get off. If you could return the car to base, that'd be fine.'

'John, I'm not sure I can find base or even our hotel, especially as it will be dark by the time we reach Pretoria.' He scratched his head, then his chin, as he sought an answer.

'The best thing to do then is follow me. I'll keep you in my sights. But remember, don't stop if you can avoid it and keep everything locked.' He was uttering the warning I had heard even before we had first come to South Africa and one which had been repeated on more than one occasion since.

The journey back went smoothly until we reached Pretoria. We made it through the outskirts with John in sight but by now it was dark and I had to make sure I was within fairly close proximity to his rear lights. As we progressed into the city, more and more cars were on the road. It became increasingly difficult to follow John despite the city lights, as other cars began to get between us.

Then came a major problem. John turned right at traffic lights and, before I could follow, cars from the opposite direction filled the junction and I became locked in behind other cars wanting to turn right. All I could do was wait, but before the cars in front of me got clear and I could go, the lights changed to red. Any slim chance I had of keeping sight of my guide had gone. By the time I managed to cross to the road taken by John he was nowhere in sight. He hadn't bothered to wait and probably assumed we were still close by. There were enough headlights to give that impression, but I had been in similar situations before, trying to follow another car, and knew that without very great care and a good deal of luck things like this were almost inevitable. All we could do was carry on and hope we would meet up with him. We crossed a couple more junctions, scanning left and right in the hope of seeing him, but we had no luck. 'We'll have to rely on the street map,' I said to Aurora. 'We've lost him.'

Aurora managed to take from her bag the map of Pretoria we had been given by the hotel receptionist and then, against all the advice, I decided to stop so that we could study it together and decide which streets to follow. With nerves on edge and regular glances along the street to make sure no-one was approaching we looked at the map and plotted a route. With almost a sigh of relief I started off in the direction the map advised. But it was never going to be as simple as that. We travelled at a slow pace. Firstly, I still hoped I would see John or possibly a police officer who could give us some advice. Secondly, I had to be sure we followed the right route and so persisted in asking Aurora to keep an eye on the map whilst reading the street signs.

What I was expecting Aurora to do was not easy. Street lighting along some of the streets was not as bright as it could have been, the map was mostly in shadow and Aurora had difficulty following both the map and the street signs at the same time. The mood with which we had settled into Mount Grace had now gone to be replaced by irritability as I called for the route on the map and the street names. Not surprisingly, Aurora was struggling to follow both and so give an accurate answer. Her difficulties were increased by the streets which bore no name signs, a not uncommon occurrence in any city, I've found, especially when you are relying on them. The result was a wandering car, too confused to go quickly, too anxious to stop. The situation was desperate!

How we got back to the hotel I'll never know, but we did, both of us perspiring from the anxiety of the drive and the dangers we imagined. I had decided sometime before we reached our goal that there was no way I was going to drive the car back to the base from which we had picked it up. I simply told the receptionist where I had left the car and asked her to contact John and get him to have the car collected. I left the car keys at reception and without bothering about what was likely to happen to the car or to John went up to our room for a shower. What a pleasure to get rid of the sweat! We then had dinner, with neither of us yet being calm enough to enable sensible conversation. Once we were back in our room we kissed and made up and then went on to finalise preparations for the next day's course.

Proteas Flower in Kirstenbosch Gardens

The Lighthouse at Cape Point

Chapman's Peak

The Sleeping Seal

Statue Commemorating Cecil Rhodes

View of Victoria and Albert

Penguins at Boulders

Woman on the move

A Zulu Village

The Tower of Pizza

Young boy on the roadside

A school

Wagons at Blood River

Zulu Hut

Spion Kop

Spion Kop

Zulu Village
Rourke's Drift Museum

Chapter 7

The Garden Route

There was a good attendance in the conference room the following day. Aurora put out the course booklets while I set up the overhead projector and the screen. I had become used to bringing my own projector from England because several venues we had been programmed to visit didn't have their own. The course relied a good deal on overhead slides but I suspect that if the worst came to the worst I could rely on the booklets I had prepared and issued.

The course participants were in a good mood and after Todd had introduced me I was able to get them to settle with, as usual, a few introductory jokes such as: Teacher, 'Why are you late?' Pupil, 'I overslept Miss.' Teacher, 'You mean you need to sleep at home too!' For their part, the course members would look up every time I used the 'u' sound and respond to my strong Yorkshire vowel by re-pronouncing the word and then having a good laugh. In my case, I couldn't resist my own usual response by uttering, in their long drawn out fashion, 'Oh...Kay...'

At the start of the course I dealt with the policy on whole-school evaluation, using the overhead projector and slides to explain the basic principles, where the different responsibilities lay and the key areas which the supervisors were required to comment on. These included the quality of teaching and learning and the effectiveness of leadership and management, not only of the principal but also of the governing body. I also stressed the need for them to keep good records of what they had done during the evaluation and of any meetings they held with school staff. I reiterated the importance of their recording their findings and presenting it in a way which would ensure the Provincial authorities would be fully aware of the strengths and weaknesses within the schools. The weekend at Mount Grace had convinced me that such clear indicators were the only way to achieve a genuine response from the authorities.

In the second session I moved on to group work in which the supervisors were asked to discuss how they would record a lesson observation and its planning and to what extent what they wrote matched the grades they may have given. It was as I was talking about keeping good records of all the information they were given that I began to wonder about the reaction in the previous course when I mentioned school documentation. I did not want to ask for too much from people who I knew had limited access to a range of necessary resources which would be regarded as normal in England. For a moment my thoughts drifted back to the day when one of my own planned visits was interrupted by the lack of transport and the references in Todd's report to the limited access the supervisors had to necessary resources such as cars. It had never struck me as an issue, and going on my experience in the United Kingdom and even Romania, it never had been. But it led me to wondering, yet again, what other elements I was introducing into whole-school evaluation which they would not, in the real world, be able to carry out. For the moment, they were enthusiastically involved in learning, making notes and asking sensible questions. They certainly gave the impression that they believed what they were hearing was possible and were committed to implementing it.

I have to say that although the courses were always treated by the trainees with great seriousness they always provided me with surprises. On this occasion, during one of the afternoon breaks, two prospective white supervisors came up to me and complimented me on working through the sessions without taking my jacket off or without removing my tie. They said they were so tired of lecturers being 'casual', as they called it, and were delighted in being on a course where the leader, 'Behaved like a course leader.' I have to admit I was flattered by the attention they had paid to my appearance, and, hoping they had been equally involved in what I had said about whole-school evaluation, thanked them for their kind words. I felt encouraged to continue in the same vein throughout the rest of the course, no matter the heat and how much I perspired.

I had planned the week with a range of plenary sessions and group work designed to deal with issues the pilots had revealed as shortcomings in what many schools did, as well as how effectively the supervisors carried out their responsibilities. Having used the early plenary sessions to go through the policy and some issues raised in the pilot evaluations, I asked the trainees to carry out tasks involving them in following the correct procedures for completing the various recording forms and writing a report on an imaginary school based on what they had recorded on the forms. I also asked them to discuss, in their groups, the best way of keeping accurate records of what they were likely to see and do during an evaluation. I used the later plenary sessions to go over some solutions but also to reiterate the importance of fulfilling commitments, whether as supervisors, facilitators or as district personnel.

At the end of the week, when the course had been completed, Aurora and I decided to extend our stay for a further few days and do what we had always wanted to do since we had started visiting South Africa, which was to follow the well publicised Garden Route. We had heard a good deal about it and were advised that it was a must for tourists on any visit to South Africa. Although we didn't yet regard ourselves as tourists, we decided to make the best of our opportunity. Why visit one of the most beautiful countries in the world and see it only as a place of work?

Todd was good enough to give us a lift into Johannesburg airport from where we flew to Port Elizabeth. This gave me the opportunity to visit St George's Cricket ground, famous for test matches, and for a short time re-live my visits to Australia's Melbourne Cricket Ground and West Indies' Queens Park Oval on Trinidad and Tobago, before we set off on our journey in a hired car. Our intention was to drive along the prescribed Garden Route to Cape Town, savouring the beauties we were promised as we passed through the well-known areas along the route. Once in Cape Town we knew we could take a plane back to the United Kingdom. We reckoned on a week's drive.

We had not studied any guide books and so our journey was to be an exploratory adventure, with our relying on a map and scraps of information we had picked up from course members. It is amazing how lunch and coffee breaks gave us an opportunity to talk to the mix of South African supervisors, black, white and coloured, about their country and about areas some of them had never had the good fortune to visit. The lives of the non-whites had been so controlled in the past that they could add little to what they could tell us about their immediate area, but from the white members we could learn much more. In the same way we learned about Little Switzerland and Mount Grace, we heard of Plettenberg Bay, Knysna, George, which offered a chance to visit the ostriches and caves at Oudshoorn, the beach at Mossel Bay and the awe-inspiring journey through the mountain passes before descending to Cape Town.

Once we had started on our journey it didn't take us long to wander off the main highway and seek what we thought might be a more interesting route along the side roads. From time-to-time, though, we came back to travelling along the highway as we sought to see how the term Garden Route had come into being.

As we had hoped, once we left the main road and went into the country we found the area so different to what we had been able to see from the highway. It is true the highway gave us views of the sea and the overlooking mountains, but it was only when we left it that we began to see houses in which owners clearly took a pride and gardens which reflected much of what we had heard about the garden route. When off the highway we passed villages with well-kept gardens and had sight of the wide variety of flora. Even so, it was essential we cut back onto the main highway regularly if only to find somewhere to stay overnight.

On that first night we found a first rate hotel in Plettenberg Bay. It was beautifully appointed, giving ready access to the beach and the sea, as well as having its own swimming pool and attractive gardens. It was the sort of place in which we found chocolate on our pillows when we entered our room and were asked, every time we passed reception, whether or not we were enjoying our stay. We booked in for two nights, which gave us the opportunity not only to wander on the beach but also an afternoon during which we were able to venture up into the town. We were keen to make the best of our stay.

When we went into town we couldn't help but be struck by the variation in quality of the different properties we passed. We were to learn over a cup of coffee in one of the bars that the town reflected some of the most saddening elements of the apartheid system. Certain parts of the town and the beach had been segregated, with much of the best being available to whites rather than to the black population. It had led to unrest and riots in the early 1990s, which, in some way, foreshadowed the changes that were to occur with the release of Nelson Mandela.

There was no doubt that everything about the hotel in which we were staying was of high quality and it was not difficult to see it as one serving the white population. Fortunately, things in South Africa had changed, but I have to admit that there was nothing in the clientele of the hotel which suggested it.

The hotel was of such quality that I should have realised, before I made a vital mistake, it was going to be costly. To be honest, when I was shown the bill it didn't look too expensive and I wondered what I had been worried about. It was only when the receptionist spoke the important words indicating the amount of rand I needed to pay that I realised I was being too optimistic. I took another and closer look at the bill and saw there was a number, almost hidden by the way it was positioned on the left of the paper, which I had not seen. The gap left between it and the second number made a significant difference to what I had to pay. I had been stupid enough to miss and ignore this first number. I kept a brave face and went through the process of paying, trying to avoid showing my real feelings. But what a shock! Aurora looked at me with the sort of pitiful look she produces when I do the sort of thing she believes she never would do, as I counted out far more money than I had anticipated. She seemed to be saying, 'Anyone with any sense would have seen what you didn't see.' I left, chastened, determined not to be caught out again.

When we left Plettenberg Bay, we continued to move along the garden route, noting the houses and gardens of what we could only assume to be those of white inhabitants. It was unlikely, we felt, that they would be those of the black population.

Our journey on the following day took us towards Wilderness, a place about which we had heard a good deal and one in which we thought we may spend the night. But in our view, the name properly fitted the area. Even so, it was here we decided to stay overnight in as cheap a bed and breakfast as we could find. Whilst the experience of Plettenberg Bay stuck long in the mind of a Yorkshireman, another stop would give the same Yorkshireman the opportunity to see how well he had remembered the way South Africans used numbers. The bed and breakfast overlooked a wide and appealing beach and we spent some time wandering across its inviting sands.

The day's journey had enabled us to enjoy the range of flora which was the delight of Aurora. The area in which we were travelling is famous for its fynbos and even I was struck by the range of flowers and their colours which the single word, fynbos, portrayed. Aurora was in her element and from time-to-time she asked me to stop so that she could cradle in her hands the flowers and smell their scent. I suspect our garden in Sardinia carries some flower or other which could be described as a memory from our trips to South Africa.

We decided to spend part of the day in the neighbouring town of Knysna, a town which we had passed through earlier on our drive. We drove back to the town and, following the suggestion in the guide book we had recently purchased, decided to take a boat trip. The calmness of the sea in the estuary enabled us to enjoy the view of the small fishing boats moving about the calm waters and the luxurious villas, seemingly hanging on to the mountain sides, which overlooked the sea. But then we met up with what the guide book described as Knysna's most famed attraction, the Knysna Heads. It was here, we were informed by our guide, that many sailing vessels had come to grief as they tried to enter the estuary. I'm pleased to write that our captain halted our boat so that we could see from a distance the rough, bumpy waters which had made the entry into Knysna Bay so treacherous. Fortunately, the captain of our boat decided against braving the turbulent waters, turned the boat and delivered us safely back to Kysna.

It was a trip we both enjoyed and felt worth making, but when we discussed it later in our bed and breakfast in Wilderness, we couldn't avoid admitting pangs of guilt about how some people find ways of enjoying the good life, whilst others would never experience it.

From Wilderness we followed the main highway to our next destination, George. It was during our time in George that we decided to make a trip out to what is described as the Ostrich world capital, Oudtshoorn. Without realising it, we found ourselves on the famous Montagu Pass, a steep winding road which took us through marvellous countryside to our destination. From the breathtaking panoramas we moved on to view the tall, gangling Ostrich, with necks as long as their legs, as they wandered about their wire fenced enclosures. I suspect many South Africans find them no more interesting than many Englishmen may find a cat or mongrel dog, but to us, seeing them strutting around their enclosure, pecking at anything they saw as a threat, they were an exhilarating sight.

After treating ourselves to an experience we would not expect to enjoy in England, we decided to drive on a little further and visit the Cango Caves. The caves I often take visitors to in Sardinia, with their wall images painted centuries ago, have nothing of the grandeur of the Cango, though there is a cave just outside Alghero in Sardinia, Neptune's Cave, which would offer good competition. Here, in South Africa, the Cango Caves were lit to enable the eyes to penetrate the high ceilings and, with varying success, the deep upper corners and the many stalactites and stalagmites. As we moved from one cave to another, we were informed of their known history by the guide, a young black girl. She was clearly enthralled with what she was doing and the tenor of her voice as she took us through the history of the caves was far distant from the often bored descriptions offered by many tour guides.

We stayed overnight in George, a town with a good deal of appeal with its magnificent Dutch Reformed Church, and oldest Anglican Cathedral and Catholic church in South Africa. Its wide streets and range of shops also encouraged us out to make an evening walk before retiring to bed after a super day.

Next morning we moved on, beyond the harbour town of Mossel Bay, the mid-point of our journey, to a small game park where we stayed for the night. It was here where a donkey approached and rubbed its nose against Aurora's window. It was obviously in search of some love and attention, but Aurora simply saw it as an obstacle to alighting from the car. For a moment or two we were stuck and the donkey persisted. We had heard a good deal about keeping car doors locked so that we were safe, but nobody had told us about how to protect ourselves from donkeys. Eventually, the donkey gave the startled Aurora room to alight from the car and rush towards reception, but the donkey, not to be outdone, simply followed us all the way up to the reception counter. It caused a good deal of mirth among the hotel staff as Aurora kept trying to move sideways from the donkey but without succeeding in shaking off its attention. She was relieved when the receptionist said, 'Not to worry. It's our welcoming donkey. It always behaves this way but never does any harm. Jack, come and take Will away.' Jack came up and led the donkey, Will, out of reception. I had followed Aurora and the donkey into reception and couldn't but be amused by what had occurred. It would be a story to tell and re-tell for years to come. Only now, some years later, does Aurora laugh about the experience.

Having booked in we made our way to a small thatched cottage which was to be our resting place for the night. As we brought in our belongings I joked about the netting over the bed which, in the way it was hanging from the ceiling, seemed to offer protection from mosquitoes through the night only to someone who stood up straight rather than lying down. After some discussion with Aurora, who pointed out the idiocy of my assumption, we managed to get everything in order so that we could have a good night's rest, lying down.

Our overnight stay, we learned, included an evening's safari. While it was still light, we were taken around the game park in an open truck. It was feeding time for the animals and the driver knew his route well. We saw lions, behind wire fencing, gorging on huge joints of meat which he threw to them, and in the distance a herd of buffalo. As usual, the impala were running in all directions. We saw zebra and the occasional elephant. It made for an interesting evening but had nothing of the grandeur of Kruger Park.

The following day we continued on our journey to the capital of Western Province and one of South Africa's three capitals, Cape Town. It was a reasonable distance and took us just over two hours. We enjoyed the journey, especially as we climbed through the mountains and had our first glimpse of the valley from Sir Lowry's Pass. High above False Bay it gave us a memorable view of the mountain road as it wound its way down to the towns below, Somerset West and Strand. Our eyes were also drawn into the distance as we sought to get our first view of our destination, Cape Town. But there were other sights we could not avoid before we settled on the capital city. We couldn't help but be shocked at the sight of the habitations sprawling beyond Somerset West and towards Cape Town.

This was our first view of Khayelitsha and Mitchells Plain, the townships created during the apartheid years for the black and coloured populations as they were driven by the white population from their habitations in

Cape Town. Having passed through the historic town of Swellendam, with its beautiful historic buildings, especially the Dutch Reformed church and its imposing clock tower, and the impressive Langeberg Mountains which backed the town, the picture which the townships presented was a shock, especially as we had spent a little time in a beautiful area by the Breede River, drawn there by Aurora's love of different flora and our hope of seeing some of the different animals associated with the area. We didn't see any zebra but we were fortunate enough to see, rushing through the bush, half a dozen rhebok, and the straight horned antelopes, probably startled by our voices. I didn't have a camera and so the memory of seeing the animals has to live in our minds rather than on plastic. But such sights are unforgettable, as, unfortunately, is the sight of Khayelitsha and Mitchells Plain.

We continued on our journey from Lowry's Pass and along the road bordering the townships. Attempts had been made to improve the quality of houses and services in recent years but it was clear there was still much to do if the black and coloured populations were to be as well housed as the white. Mitchell's Plane and Khayelitsha typified attempts made to improve the living conditions, but as yet there had been too little time for the new Government to make any significant changes. The proximity of the habitations and the large number of people who had been crowded into them resulted in an untidiness which suggested to us pre-Mandela times.

The sight of the townships also reminded us of a visit we had made to Soweto on one of our earlier trips to

Johannesburg. As if we were tourists, we had booked a trip from the hotel and were picked up by a taxi and taken the short distance to the renowned township. The black taxi driver had his own route and nothing we were likely to say was going to encourage him to divert. He had obviously made the trip many times and from the nods and waves he got as he passed groups of people he was well known. I must say I felt uncomfortable as we made this trip. I suppose we were only making it because it was one of those that had to be made if you visited Johannesburg. But the thought of travelling through a township looking at people and their homes, rather like looking into a zoo, was disturbing. I didn't feel much better as we passed street after street of impoverished houses and saw one group of black people after another standing at the street corners.

The only sign of excitement was when we reached Nelson Mandela's former home. Its popularity was obvious and clearly denoted by the dancing and singing by a small group of locals seeking to collect money for their efforts. The taxi stopped for a while, giving me time to take rand from my pocket and put it into the bucket left for that express purpose, and then the driver moved us on to another of his targets, a shebeen owned by a lady he clearly knew well. Here, we were invited to drink and have some local food. Unused to the taste of what must have been traditional food, we found it difficult to eat and were somewhat embarrassed by the owner's question, 'Did you enjoy lunch, Sir?'

The taxi driver then took us to the disturbing memorial of the thirteen-year-old black youngster,

Hector Pietersen, who had been shot by police during the violent 1976 demonstration. The demonstration had been organised by students resisting the laws which declared they had to learn Afrikaans and use that language along with English in their studies It was the most moving of all the sights we saw in Soweto and an event which I remember being reported sometime previously by a shocked newspaper editor in England. The report had also contained a more than moving photograph of the wounded boy, his head hanging loosely over an arm, being carried by a distraught African, with his young sister running at his side.

I quietly sighed with relief when the taxi driver eventually pointed his taxi in the direction of Johannesburg and left behind what was for me one of the worst visits we had made in South Africa. The sights we had seen flooded over and almost drowned out our memory of seeing Nelson Mandela's former house, with dancing Africans providing entertainment in the street at its front.

We could take a view about apartheid, either seeing it as an inevitable and to some extent justifiable consequence of one tribe wanting to maintain control over the others, or as a cruel and harsh system imposed because of the disdain one group of people had for another. As we knew, tribal rivalries had always existed in Africa, a continent on which history seems to unfold through one tribe seeking to dominate another. But was the history of the United Kingdom any different? I couldn't help thinking of the differences in wealth which have existed in England through history and how sections of the people have been exploited for the benefit of others. The row of white stones we had photographed on Spion Kop and the memorials in Ladysmith were still strong in my mind. To what extent, I couldn't help wonder, did the sacrifices of those young men, who probably never really knew where South Africa was, contribute to the grand houses and their prized contents which can be seen in many areas of England today?

As we had journeyed along the minor roads, just off the route advised by the guide book, and then the highway, neither Aurora nor I could help but feel a sense of guilt for being able to afford to do what we were now able to do. But, like those of wealth in previous times, I suspect we felt it better to forget those who were less fortunate and thank the good fortune which was enabling us to enjoy what South Africa had to offer.

When we eventually arrived in Cape Town, we decided to contact our friends who lived in Hout Bay, an area we were to find was so different from the townships, and certainly Soweto. By following the directions they gave us we found our way from Cape Town to their house without too much difficulty. The house was, as I expected, situated on a well-tended estate and in an area inhabited by the white population. We stayed with them for a couple of nights and had the pleasure of being taken up towards Chapman's Peak, from which we had a fantastic view of Hout Bay and the surrounding mountains. Little wonder there were those who sought to protect it from change and cherished the memorial, which read *'The construction of Chapman's Peak Drive started in 1915 as a narrow winding gravel road and after seven years work the same drive, 'hewn out of the face of sheer mountains' was officially opened by the Governor General of the then Union of South Africa, Prince Arthur of Connaught'.*

After our second night with our friends we moved back to the airport in Cape Town. We returned the car and boarded the plane back to Heathrow without having any real opportunity to enjoy the famous sites of Cape Town. They would have to await another visit. We had seen a great deal of South Africa, however, and had stories, such as those involving our visit to Spion Kop and those relating to the social and educational differences, which we could take back with us to England and share with our friends.

Chapter 8

KwaZulu Natal

By the end of March, 2001, whilst I was back in England, Todd was able to send me a more detailed report of the pilot evaluations. It led to me to giving further thought to the training framework to ensure I covered matters which had not gone well in the pilot. Fortunately, there was enough in Todd's report to suggest that the whole-school evaluation policy was suitable enough for purpose and the areas identified for evaluation were appropriate. The report also reinforced my feeling that the changes I had already made to the training framework and which I had introduced during the course on my previous visit to South Africa were appropriate. I concluded the revised framework and course would serve their purpose in ensuring all supervisors operated within the same principles, produced evaluations which were of similar type and rigour across the different Provinces, and could provide a national picture of the quality of education.

The common approach I and the National Directorate were seeking could, I knew, only result from the quality of training I provided. It had to be supervisors that would provide clear and perceptive evaluations based on well-substantiated and valid judgements. I came to the conclusion that this was especially important in relation to teaching and learning. But I knew that as yet, South Africa had not developed a strong enough national system of measuring pupils' achievements across all stages of their education to enable supervisors to measure and compare pupils' progress with any real confidence. This shortcoming existed despite there being reference in the National Policy on whole-school evaluation of 2001 of the need for *'measurable levels of achievement that learners should reach in their academic, physical and personal development.'*

I worked hard with a group of trainees in Gauteng Province before moving on to Durban in Kwa-ZuluNatal. Aurora had been with me in Johannesburg and now came with me to Durban on a journey by mini-bus which took us eight hours, a journey which brought home to me more clearly than a map would, how large South Africa is. Throughout the drive we were entertained by our companions in Xhosa, so could do no more than view the country through which we passed or close our eyes for some sleep. The national route, N3, took us through the Drakensberg Mountains within the vicinity of Harrismith, which brought back memories of Little Switzerland and the non-consecrated Mass, past Pietermaritzburg and on to Durban.

I had visited Durban with Todd on a previous trip to South Africa and had met up with some of the senior officers in the Province. They had been welcoming then and were even more so now. They expressed their delight that I had crossed to Durban and were sure the training would be beneficial to the new supervisors. I exchanged handshakes and smiles, knowing their welcome was genuine. On the first morning of the course, Aurora and I finished breakfast and then went into the conference room.

We went through our usual routine as we prepared the room for training and awaited the arrival of the trainees. There had been a time when some, and probably most, would have arrived up to half an hour late for sessions. It seemed to be the South African way. I had appealed on a couple of occasions for punctuality, but my efforts had been largely ignored. I spoke with Todd about it and he could do no more than shrug his shoulders. It was as if he were saying, '*That's how it always is in South Africa.*' Whether it was a reflection on the attitudes of black and coloured Africans I was never sure, because there was no guarantee that all the white Africans would be present at the start of a session either.

As my appeals for promptness had failed, I did what I had had to do on occasions in England. I informed the trainees I would start the session at the correct time, whether anyone was there or not. I fully expected to be talking to an empty room at the beginning of my next session. But, thank goodness, the threat worked. And so, from the earliest days, the course members gradually got into the habit of arriving at the published time. They knew what to expect. If they wished to get everything they wanted from the course they had to be there at the beginning of each session. There were no repeats. And so, in Durban, as everywhere else, I started on time and everyone was present. Amazing how the word had spread.

It was fortunate Aurora came with me. Having been given a long list of trainees by the Provincial officers of Kwa-ZuluNatal, we prepared the room for about one-hundred-and-fifty. It was just as I was about to begin the first morning session that another group of trainees burst through the door. I couldn't believe what was happening. I recognised the earliest of the newcomers. They were supervisors whom I had recently finished training in Gauteng. Impressed by what they had experienced, they told me they had made such a long journey from Johannesburg to be present in Durban because, 'We enjoyed the previous session in Jo'burg and wanted to reinforce what we had learned by joining the course in Durban.' I could do no other than welcome them and nod to Aurora to provide desks, seats and training materials for them. She was supported by Provincial and hotel staff. Without much delay and admiring their efforts to travel from Johannesburg to be on time in Durban, I was able to get the course under way.

I worked hard at seeking to fill in the gaps in training which had obviously been present in previous courses, again ensuring that the trainees were meticulous in completing forms, particularly when they were tackling group tasks, and understood the importance of recording clearly the activities they had undertaken and how effectively they were supporting their judgements. I stressed this was particularly true when it came to recording lesson observations and that they should always ensure identified weaknesses and strengths were properly documented when referring to teaching and the learning. Accepting the fact that there was no national system of assessing pupils, I advised them to make use of pupils' notebooks and their conversations with them to establish how well they were progressing in their learning, year by year. This, I assured them, would help in any feedback to the teacher and to the principal.

I felt the day's sessions went well and was pleased with the feedback from participants. When I got back to our room I decided I needed to modify the group tasks for the next day so as to broaden their value, but before that I thought Aurora and I should get some fresh Indian Ocean air into our lungs by walking along the sea front. The usual happened as we walked past reception, 'Take care, Sir. Parts of Durban can be dangerous.' Consequently, we kept to the road which followed the wide, inviting beach and occasionally moved down onto sand which, presumably uncovered by sea water for some time, was hard and crisp. In the distance we could see surf boarders testing the waves and trying out their ability to ride them with varying success.

For Aurora and me, the walk was effort enough and provided pleasant relaxation after the intensity of running a day's training for almost two-hundred participants. The skyscraper hotels and commercial buildings rose up on our left and the beach and Ocean drew our eyes to the right. I think we both wondered what had happened in our lives to bring us to such a beautiful place so far from where we were born. No doubt there were others, especially the many Asians we saw, who probably had similar thoughts, but many of those were here because of less acceptable reasons than ours. One thing we had become increasingly aware of on our walk was the number of Asians in the city, a reminder of its proximity to India and the importation of many from the East to work on the land. I squeezed Aurora's hand as I realised our good fortune.

Aware of the warning and my need to think through the next day's training sessions we were back in our room in just under the hour. As the evening darkened, the lights came on and we could enjoy a different view of Durban's seafront from our tenth-floor window. There was more movement than had been the case earlier in the evening and it seemed as though lots of people, black, white and coloured, were on their way to places of enjoyment.

I was training in Durban for a week, each of the five days having four sessions. Fortunately, I had spent my time in England profitably and had prepared well. What I hadn't foreseen, however, was the difficulty I was to have on the second day with the overhead projector. As luck would have it, Aurora and I were in the conference room well before the trainees. I followed my customary routine and I took the opportunity to line up the projector and screen. I switched on. Nothing! I couldn't understand it. A quiet panic began to rumble in my stomach. What was I going to do without the projector? Aurora became aware of my problem and quickly went for the hotel's technician. What he did I have no idea, but before long we were back in business. The nerves eased, the trainees came in and the course began.

On this occasion I not only had the overheads to worry about but I also had a couple of videos I wanted to show. One was of a lesson, set in an English school, which I wanted the trainees to discuss. Fortunately, during the session in which I had planned to introduce this exercise, everything worked to perfection and I was able to show it on the big screen. The trainees had a series of questions to answer as they watched, their responses to which they were to discuss in groups. We then had a plenary to see what had been noted and learned. This led to questions which still had to be resolved nationally. *How do we measure achievement? How do we know children are doing well? How do educators know their teaching is being effective?* It contributed to what I wanted the future supervisors to recognise – any lesson needed careful scrutiny and to be recorded properly. But it also highlighted the problem for evaluators when there was, as yet, no national system of assessing pupils' progress. As the reader will realise, the focus of the training followed on from Todd's summary of the pilot evaluations and the difficulty some of the supervisors had in matching their grades to the notes they had recorded and the probability that what they had written and the grade they had given was not a fair reflection of what they had seen. The group session revealed that most of the trainees still had much to learn.

After helping with setting out the conference room, Aurora said she would go back to our room and take the opportunity to read something from the books she had brought with her. It was only when we met at lunchtime she told me what she really did. She decided, against all advice, to go into Durban, shopping. As she told the story, I couldn't help see at least some embarrassment on her face. 'I didn't get very far when I felt I was being followed. There was one chap behind me and I'm sure he was following me. I thought I saw another across the street doing the same. I stopped at different places, pretending to look in shop windows, and I saw they stopped. Phew, Terry, I became more and more worried.' I looked at her and my face must have revealed total disbelief at what she was telling me. *'How could she do it again?'* The answer wasn't far away. *'It was so typically Aurora!'*

'I tried to walk faster, but each time I looked around they were still there. Thanks are to God I saw a policeman standing on one of the corners. I went up to him, asked him if he would talk to me and then told him about the men following me. I told him I had nothing of value so what did they hope to get? He simply said, 'Of course you have. You have that gold cross round your neck. That would be of value to them.' He looked down the street at the men. They'd stopped and were looking a bit shifty, and then he said to me, 'You shouldn't be on the street alone. Where's your hotel?' I told him and he said, 'Go back there straight away. Forget the shopping.'

For once, Aurora did as she was told and, clearly frightened, she came straight back to the hotel. 'Thanks be to God, the policeman walked just behind me and I got back here safe and sound.'

'What on earth were you thinking, Aurora? All these warnings and you still do it.' I couldn't restrain the frustration in my voice, and feared my words would do no more than have the usual effect. Knowing her as I did, I knew she would still do what she wanted, no matter how many warnings she had. But, on this occasion, she had heeded the advice of a stranger in uniform and I had every hope it would make her aware of the dangers as well as the significance of the advice we were being given in every hotel we stayed.

Fortunately, Aurora's shopping trip into Durban had provided a learning experience for her. For the rest of the week I was able to relax, knowing she was unlikely to repeat her first day's experience. It was only when the sessions were finished that we took time to venture together into Durban again and learn something of the fascinating city it is. Built as it is on the Indian Ocean it is not difficult to see why it reflects both colonial and Asian influences. It became a stopping place for colonial shipping on its way to India and China, and a port of entry for labourers from India. My history lessons in England taught me that large numbers were transported from India to work on the sugar plantations and at the end of the nineteenth century Mahatma Ghandi had unsuccessfully led resistance to the treatment of his countrymen.

As we wandered along the beach front we both wondered how the Asians had fared in the age of apartheid and how they were treated now, in the first years of the twenty-first century. We certainly saw plenty of Asians as we took our evening walks and could see in the shops we passed how well they were catered for. We also saw plenty of white people, many, no doubt, able to trace their ancestry to those brave men who were prepared to make the dangerous trip around the Cape of Good Hope. White, black, coloured and Asian had much of a past to reflect upon.

I knew I had worked hard along with Aurora to provide good quality training in Durban. It was only at the end of the week's course that I learned how successful I had been. It is never easy for a course leader to know how well he is being received by those he is seeking to train or to know whether their nods of approval and 'Thanks' mean any more than that, and so it came as a great surprise when, after the final session, a young Zulu course member suddenly took the stage. He bore a shield and a spear and to the cheers of the course members went through a Zulu war dance. It was tremendously exciting to watch his rising exhilaration as the rest of the course members began to move and sway to the beating of his shield. It was as if he had taken the drug the Zulus were reputed to take before a battle. There is no doubt I would not have liked to have faced up to him in the mood he was displaying. When he had finished he came across and politely presented me with the shield and spear. That was not all. I was also given several complimentary cards, clearly bought locally and bearing welcoming images of Zulu as on the image of the card below, which had been signed by the trainees.

The comments on the card below provide examples of the trainees' response:

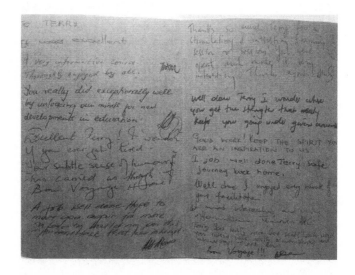

Others were also glowing in their praise, containing words such as: *'You really empowered us,' 'Excellent presentation,' 'You were very good and you need to be in SA for us for keeps',*

The last of these three comments is interesting in light of what I had been discussing with the National Directorate in the weeks previously. I had begun to discuss with Todd and Dr Mgijima the possibility of staying in South Africa for a period of two to three years. My concern was that although the supervisors were learning skills, there was no one, because of the Provincial system, in overall charge; no one able to lead the supervisors and facilitators nationally. In addition, there was no-one in a position to amend the framework for whole-school evaluation in response to any likely changes in the education system. Those of us closely involved knew there was still much to do to ensure the policy was properly implemented and sustained.

The negotiations between the interested parties, the officials at the Centre for British Teachers and those from the National Directorate, went on for some months and it looked as though the proposal for me to stay in South Africa over a more permanent period was more than likely. I was keen and so was Aurora. The discussions apparently concerned the type of house we might have, where it was likely to be situated, and the means of transport which would be made available to us. But then discussions suddenly came to a halt. I was not to be offered a long-term contract and nobody ever explained to me why. Such are the foibles of consultancy!

This meant a continuation of the regular journeys to and from South Africa and being available as each Province requested training or the Quality Assurance Department wanted the evaluation of schools monitoring. It meant continuing to visit areas in South Africa which I and Aurora would never have visited as one-off tourists. To go to Limpopo, which had been called Northern Province until the South Africans changed its name in 2003 so that it fitted more suitably with the locality through which the Limpopo River flowed, Nelspruit in Mpumalanga, a city in the North East of South Africa on what was called the Crocodile River, Pietermaritzburg, founded by the Boers after the defeat of the Zulu Dingane at Blood River in KwaZulu-Natal, and Bloemfontein, another remnant of the days of the Boertrekkers, a city which blended the new and the old in the Free State, presented us with journeys and sights which live in the memory and helped us understand so much more about South Africa.

Of course, work did not cease when I was back in England. Not only did I have to think about my commitments in South Africa and continue to work on different aspects of training and the conduct of whole-school evaluation, I had to think of my own role as a team leader on school inspections, Ofsted, Independent and Diocesan, in England. They were commitments which kept me abreast of innovations in the education system in England and ensured I was in a good position to use my expertise elsewhere.

It was, in fact, during one of my periods back in England that I was asked to travel to Montenegro to help in re-writing the country's policy on education. Keen to keep pace with what was happening in Europe, the Education Department of Montenegro looked to England to supply the expertise. It was interesting to find the people I worked with somewhat more intransigent than the Romanians and the South Africans. I was never sure whether or not it was the outcome of the strong communist ethic which seemed to linger in their thinking. I was in Montenegro for no more than a week, but during that time I worked with officials looking at their revisions of the state's education policy, and got to know a good deal about a country which had recently been involved in war. The evidence of it was only too real when, having asked to go to Mass on the Sunday of my visit, I was taken out of Podgorica, the capital and a centre of the Orthodox faith, to an outlying village with a Catholic church. The car journey took us through areas which still contained shelled and bombed ruins. I was shocked to see that significant areas of the hinterland still bore the scars of war.

It was during my stay in Montenegro that my trigeminal nerve struck again. The symptoms caused the excruciating pain which I experienced from time-to-time, kept me awake at nights and refused to let me chew anything I was given. It was with some uncertainty that I accepted an invitation from my hosts to visit a restaurant for lunch. Fearful of having anything which would need chewing I went for what I thought would be a soft sheet of pasta, well-cooked meat and sauce. It led me to having the worst lasagne I had ever had in my life. Somehow, I managed through the week and helped the particular official from the education department to review and revise the education policy in readiness for its presentation to the government.

When I returned to England I was able to get some treatment for my problem, but its re-emergence from time-to-time was something of which I remained constantly aware and which was to affect me on one of my trips to South Africa.

Chapter 9

Rustenburg and Pilanisberg

When I got back to England I found Todd had sent on information concerning a request by North West Province for some training for their new supervisors. It was to be based in Rustenburg, a town North East of Johannesburg. It was to be a place I was to hear more of when the England football team made it their base for the 2010 World Cup in South Africa.

In those early years of the century I knew little of it. It was only when I began to dip into its history that I learned of its importance and possibly why it had been chosen by the Province as the location for the course.

Rustenburg had started its life as an agricultural town surrounded by farms producing a wide variety of produce including citrus fruit, peanuts, maize and wheat. It was also well known for its herds of cattle. It had been the town in which Paul Kruger, one-time President of the South African Republic, had had his home and as such became a key area for the Boers and one of their oldest settlements after the Great Trek. Apparently, the town earned its name in earlier times because once the Boers had conquered the African tribes with whom they had to contest ownership, they believed they could rest in the town, Rustenburg meaning 'resting town' in Afrikaans. The peace the Boers had looked for did not last long, as the town's proximity to Mafeking, a place I had already visited, meant it had been drawn into the second Boer War in 1899.

Later, in 1929, the discovery of platinum transformed the town from any semblance of the peaceful environment sought by the early settlers to one invaded by those seeking wealth and who were prepared to turn the town into one of industry.

Todd picked me up at Johannesburg airport and we headed for Rustenburg. The Province did us proud by providing us with accommodation in a very well appointed hotel. It was in a rural setting, set back against what I came to know as the Magaliesberg mountain range.

As we drove through the town, I was struck by the flowering of the large number of jacaranda trees which lined its streets. The hotel overlooked the town and provided a good view of the valley beyond. I felt it was an ideal location for the course.

The trainees showed their usual enthusiasm, never failing to remind me of their amusement at my pronunciation of 'budget', or 'books'. They were keen to learn, however, and responded well to the tasks they were set. Everything proceeded well until the morning one of the trainees came from his room to inform the rest of us the astounding news, 'When I woke up this morning, I found a snake on my bed!' Before I could even begin the session that morning there was a mass exodus. The trainees rushed back to their bedrooms to make sure they had not suffered the same fate by ignoring the warnings of the hotel not to leave any windows open. I wasn't far behind!

Once the group had re-assembled I moved forward with the course. In the first session I focused on what I regarded as the fourfold purposes of evaluating schools. First, I wanted the trainees to recognise the importance of evaluating what I described as the quality of educational provision in individual schools; second, I sought to help them identify the key factors which would help the different schools improve their effectiveness; third, I drew their attention to the need to pull together their reports on the individual schools that had been evaluated throughout the Province into one report so that the Provincial and National authorities were given an overview of strengths and shortcomings of education in the Province and could see what action they should be taking if the principles of Tirisano were to be achieved; and fourth, knowing that the course members reflected a cross section of representatives from different Provinces, I sought to raise their recognition of who was accountable for what at different levels in the education system. I emphasised the importance of the Provincial officers being aware of these basic purposes and that if they did what they could in response to the information provided by well-substantiated evaluations, they should see an improvement in the overall quality of education within the Province.

I sought to personalise what I was saying by drawing the trainee's attention to my own experiences when visiting different schools and different types of school in South Africa, ensuring I didn't minimise the problems which some, for example the farm schools, faced. This led naturally, in my next presentation, to my outlining the nine areas contained in the national whole-school evaluation policy on which supervisors were expected to report. The rest of the week was concerned either with the trainees tackling issues in groups or my explaining what the policy intended. We considered aspects such as the basic functionality of the school, the quality of leadership, management and communication within a school, curriculum provision and resources, the quality of teaching and learning, the levels of achievement attained by the pupils, their overall educational development, and links with the school established with parents and the wider community. These, I indicated, were examples taken from the nine areas for evaluation identified in the national policy on whole-school evaluation and which should be key to guiding them in the range of areas they needed to consider when carrying out their responsibilities within a school

.

Inevitably, questions arose as the trainees began to explore the issues surrounding the nine areas and their implications for their work in greater depth. They were not sure, for example, what was meant by 'basic funcionality' or how they were to judge 'learner achievement'. They were absolutely right to draw attention to the latter, because, as I mentioned earlier, there was nothing at that time in South Africa which reflected what was becoming increasingly important in England – the outcomes of standard assessment tasks designed to show what progress pupils were making year by year. It would only be much later, and with the bedding in of whole-school evaluation, that the supervisors would have some external means of assessing levels of achievement.

As for the former, basic functionality, almost their only viable models of functional schools were the Senior 'C' schools, which had continued to absorb a large proportion of the educational budget. It was generally agreed by the trainees that most of the public schools, and especially those available to black, coloured and farm children, were still under-resourced in many areas and so had little possibility of providing the quality of education as sought by Tirisano. The trainees contributed effectively to the discussions and were clearly grasping the importance their evaluations could have on moving forward educational provision throughout the country. This became evident during the discussions at lunchtime, which tended to centre on the morning's topics and provide opportunities for further questions to be asked and explored.

It was also during lunch, in general conversation with the trainees, I learned of a nearby game park. Pilanisberg was close by and some of the trainees suggested it offered the opportunity of seeing the 'Big Five'. I knew Aurora would be attracted by the possibility of a visit to a game park, even if it meant another meeting with a donkey, and so I stored the information for future reference.

The trainees' talk of Sun City, which was near the game park, left me with different feelings. Never a gambler and never wanting to be, I was put off by the comparison to Las Vegas. I knew plenty of people who would have enjoyed a visit but it was not for me. Perhaps I was wrong and perhaps there was more to Sun City than I picked up from the conversations, but I was not attracted to the idea of a visit and I was pretty sure Aurora would be of the same mind.

Not surprisingly, on Aurora's next visit to South Africa we decided to spend the weekend between courses at the Pilanisberg Game Park. I booked through the tour operator in the Holiday Inn in Pretoria for the Saturday and Sunday. The arrangements were ideal. We were to be picked up from the hotel and taken to Pilanisberg and then returned to Pretoria on the Sunday evening. We were joined by several other tourists of different nationalities as full of anticipation as we were about what we were likely to see. None of them had been to Kruger Park and for some of them this was their first visit to a game park of any sort. There was nothing like the chatter on this bus which had typified our journey on the one to Kruger. You could sense the excitement, but not the familiarity.

When we drove into Pilanisberg we were taken to the lodge in which we were staying that night. We were given time to drop off our belongings and have a quick lunch before being taken on our first trip around the park. Our driver was somewhat bolder than the one who took us around Kruger. The first time he came across a bull elephant crossing the road, he called out 'D'you want some fun?' and before anyone could respond proceeded to sound the vehicle's horn. The elephant looked up as if startled, turned, and through its seemingly too small eyes peered down the road at us. It lifted its trunk, gave a huge elephant bellow and began to move towards us. You could sense the growing panic in the mini-bus as the elephant came nearer and nearer, its huge ears flapping in anger. At the last moment, and to everyone's relief, the driver went into reverse and sped back down the road, well out of the elephant's reach. Realising its hopes of an attack were receding, the elephant lost interest, turned, and continued on its way across the road and into the bush, followed by others we took to be its family.

That was not our only experience of the day. A short time later we saw a number of zebra. The animals were running in different directions and clearly in panic. Some of our passengers, excited, stood to try to see what was causing the alarm. An unfortunate zebra suddenly broke from the group. It was being chased by two lions. It didn't get very far before one of the lions had it by its mane and managed to pull it to the ground. Two lions were now about to have their lunch! Everyone was shocked at the sight, a fact revealed by the topics of conversation as we continued on our tour, but could do no more than recognise it was how things worked in the jungle.

A short time later the driver headed up a slope which brought us to what he knew to be an excellent viewing point. He invited us out of the bus to enjoy what was around us. I'm not sure how many of the passengers alighted with confidence, knowing they were still in an area in which roamed dangerous animals. I certainly had tingles of anxiety, but realised the view was too appealing to miss and so followed his lead. We were backed by the Magaliesberg range of mountains as we stood on the hillock which gave us a superb view of the valley which stretched out before us.

The driver had been right in describing the vegetation as beautiful. As we had driven through the game park he had drawn our attention to the several distinct types to be found in the Pilanesberg. We were fortunate enough to be in the park when we could see them in full colour. He had pointed out red bushwillow, hook thorn, wild pear and buffalo thorn, and told us how each took a position on the hillsides which provided the appropriate amount of sunshine or moisture most suited to their growth. Now we were standing on the hillock and able to look in different directions, he pointed out an even wider range of vegetation which included the strange sounding umbrella thorn, karee and tamboti.

We became more excited when he went on to say that Pilanisberg contained 'The Big Five'. Along with what I'd heard from the trainees in Rustenburg about 'The Big Five', Aurora and I were now convinced that Kruger was not the only the game park to visit if we wanted to see 'The Big Five'. We had been unfortunate in Kruger not to see all five, the leopard had escaped us, but to our surprise here was another chance. We had already seen the lion and elephant, and, as we stood on our outpost, the driver drew our attention to a herd of African buffaloes quietly munching their way across the flat land below. 'To be honest,' the driver said, 'the Big Five are not natural inhabitants of Pilanisberg. They have been brought in to increase the Park's attraction and have settled well in the bushland, breeding and increasing their numbers. With luck, we'll see the other two as we travel around.' He paused to give us time to take in what he had to say and then added, 'Time to get back into the bus.' We drove further through the Park, still full of anticipation, but disappointingly had no luck with 'The Big Five'.

When we got back to the lodge we had a meal and then Aurora and I had a walk around what was a small settlement of lodges. In no time we were joined by several monkeys, interested in what we were doing, no doubt, but probably more interested in what we might throw to them. It seemed as though the monkeys, the type we had no idea, lived locally and looked to the visitors for their tit-bits. They were all over the place.

The following morning we made another trip into the Park. The driver was keen for us to see as much as we could as he followed the winding road up and over the hill we had viewed from on the previous day. Suddenly he stopped. 'There's another one,' he said. In the bush, seemingly guarding its family, was a rhinoceros. It looked at us suspiciously, obviously came to the conclusion that we were no danger, and then proceeded to relieve itself. The gush of water continued for much longer than anyone of us expected and, as the bus remained stationary, all we could do was watch and take photographs. Eventually, the rhinoceros snorted, finished what it was doing, turned to its family and moved off, its actions causing laughter and comments among the passengers in the bus.

But even more laughter resulted from what we saw next. We arrived opposite a fairly steep incline just at the same time as a couple of giraffes. The driver stopped and said, 'Watch this.' As he did so, one of the giraffes began to come down the slope. It spread its legs as wide as it could in an effort to keep its balance, but to say it stumbled down the slope, one unsteady step after the other, would be an overestimate of the sight which I wish I could have caught on video. The amount of comment in the bus added to the unimaginable sight. 'You're seeing how other animals hunt giraffe,' said the driver. 'They're pretty quick overland, but get them on a slope and...' He'd said enough. We could all see what his next words were likely to be.

Sad to report, but we never did see a leopard on our travels through the game parks. Our only option was to visit a zoo later in our South African journeys in which leopards, white and spotted, were caged. They were impressive animals, slim yet powerful and renowned for their speed. It is said that they have such power in their legs they can jump over an elephant. No matter, to this day, we have not seen one in the wild. Noted as being nocturnal animals, I suspect our only chance of seeing one would have been on a very early morning safari, but that was not to be.

Chapter 10

Progress in Western Province

It was when I was in England I received news that Todd was ill and in hospital. Fortunately, I was due in South Africa the following week and I was determined to take the opportunity to go and see him. We had struck up a solid friendship and he was a man I greatly admired. I had visited him socially and met his family – his wife and two children. I had also met his two brothers, to whom I was introduced when Todd invited me to dinner on an occasion when I was in Pretoria. Like Todd, the brothers had been involved in the struggle against apartheid and, in consequence, one now held a senior position in the military whilst the other had a senior post in administration.

On the occasion Todd invited me to dinner at his house so that I could meet his brothers and their wives, I remember being drawn into a discussion about the days of apartheid and indicating my schooldays' support for the cause of the black and coloured South Africans. During the conversation, I asked a question which has always worried me. I suppose it is because none of us knows how we are likely to respond in extreme situations. For instance, would we always stand back to let a mother and child escape from a sinking ship if we knew that such an action would result in our own death? Or would we be willing to stand forward, admit our guilt, and so volunteer to be severely punished in place of a person we knew to be innocent, if given the choice? I have to say, I find the answers difficult, though as I sit here writing I hope I would do the right thing.

I have similar thoughts about how I might have acted had I lived in South Africa at the time of apartheid. I could not help but introduce into the discussion with Todd and his brothers the question, 'I wonder what I'd have done if I'd lived in South Africa during the time of apartheid?' The response of all three brothers was immediate. 'You'd have had no choice.'

Their answer was not a surprise, I suppose, but worrying nevertheless. I suppose I knew there were options, which I had learned during the conversations I had had with a white South African who had been a colleague of mine when I was a senior lecturer in history at Trinity and All Saints Colleges way back in the early 1970s. She had been forced to leave South Africa because of her opposition to apartheid and as she put it, 'It was either that or jail.' So I reckoned I would have had one of three options – acquiesce and join the privileged, go to jail along with others who felt apartheid was unjust, or leave the country and possibly stir up opposition to white supremacy. To this day, and despite the good relationships I had with so many black and coloured South Africans as a result of my work, I am still not sure which I would have chosen had I lived in

South Africa during the 1960s and '70s, and whether the implied answer of my new friends was the one I would have had to take.

I'm pleased to say I must not have said anything during that evening to upset the brothers because on a later visit to South Africa, and before Todd's illness, I was invited to go with them and Todd as a VIP guest to watch France play a friendly football match with South Africa at Ellis Park. I was treated to drinks and food and had a grandstand view of the game, which, sadly, like most friendlies didn't produce the excitement the huge crowd was looking for. There were moments of exquisite football by both sides, but it seemed inevitable that the game would end in a rather tame draw. But for me, the whole experience was thoroughly enjoyable and introduced me to the significance of the changes looked for in post Mandela South Africa. Black and white mixed harmoniously as they urged on the national team and in the VIP lounge shared the nibbles and drinks.

Not surprisingly, I was anxious to show support for Todd in his illness and so I took an early flight to South Africa on my next visit. When I reached Pretoria I learned Todd, because of his illness, had been replaced and so I now had to relate to a new member of the National Directorate. It was during discussions with Paul, Todd's replacement, I learned of Western Cape's request for me to visit Cape Town to train their new supervisors. Linda Rose, a senior member of the Western Cape education department, who had attended one of the earlier courses in Gauteng Province, had at last persuaded her superiors of the need to introduce whole-school evaluation and to have the Province's supervisors trained so that it was implemented effectively and in common with the nationally agreed framework. For me, it meant making a journey from Pretoria to Cape Town and the possibility of piloting the use of the facilitators I had trained earlier to be the trainers of supervisors in the new system.

But first, I needed to go to see Todd, who was, I learned, in hospital and seriously ill. I went with his wife to the hospital in Pretoria, where he was in his own room and receiving some first-rate attention. However, it was clear he was very ill and unable to concentrate very much on what was being said. His nurses intimated that he would have difficulty recovering from his illness and would need a lot of support to help him do so. I knew he would get all the support he needed from his wife and children but what I saw of him led me to doubt whether it would be enough. I couldn't understand how the strong, robust Todd I had known could become so frail in such a short time.

I said the usual things one says when visiting a sick person in hospital, 'Glad to see you,' 'Hope you get well soon,' 'How are they treating you?' but I wondered if he would ever be well enough to cope with the pressure of the work in which he had been so involved and to which he had been so committed – the principle of equality was so important to him. I hoped he would recover but the condition in which I found him made me doubt it. His wife, whom he had met when fighting the cause in Swaziland, was extremely worried and though I didn't meet them on this occasion, I suspect her concerns were shared by their children. I promised I would come to see him again before I left for England.

Before I returned to England I had several commitments. One was to pull together the various reports from the different Provinces into what everyone hoped would become an annual whole-school evaluation report to the Education Minister. The motives of those in the National Directorate of Quality Assurance who supported the idea were simple. They wanted to put together as much evidence as they could about the difficulties being faced by many schools and then present it to the Ministry and to the Provincial authorities. Their aim was to demonstrate the differences in provision throughout South Africa and encourage the authorities to find the resources which education needed if the equality spoken of in Tirisano was to be achieved.

A good many more evaluations of schools had been carried out in the different Provinces since the piloting of whole-school evaluation. As a result, I had 224 school reports from six of the nine Provinces to pull together into an overall report. It meant hours of work, but satisfaction that so many schools had accepted and undergone an external evaluation. It promised well for the future.

When I had completed the report, it was submitted to the Minister of Education, Professor Kadar Asmal. The Minister wrote a forward thanking all those who had contributed to the report and stating that it should '*serve as an invaluable source of affirmation for what is good in our education system and provide inspiration for all those involved in education at National and Provincial level to tackle the challenges head on.'*

The strengths he referred to were included in the overall report. They were: the quality of much of the teaching observed; pupils' behaviour overall; the breadth of the curriculum in most schools; the willingness of citizens to serve on governing bodies; and the relationships being maintained by many schools with external agencies. The key challenges he recognised were related to the sometimes poor quality of school leadership; the limited opportunities for training of staff at all levels; the difficulties teachers had in estimating pupils' levels of achievement and progress because of the lack of secure assessment guidelines; the poor marking of pupils' work; and the provision for pupils with special educational needs. In addition, he drew attention to the references in the report to the unacceptable infrastructure and amenities in over half of the schools evaluated, concerns which he was aware were shared by many parents, mainly because they were a threat to the health, safety and security of the pupils.

The report had served its purpose and produced evidence of the shortcomings which were still present in the education system. Not all the Provinces had been involved in the pilots, however, and until they were it would be difficult to argue that such reports were truly national.

Aurora had not been with me when I went to see Todd but she had been with me when we spoke to Paul. She was as pleased as I was to hear about the news from Western Cape, mainly because she knew how disappointed I had been at the Province's non-involvement with whole-school evaluation. For both of us, another trip to Cape Town, a city which we knew was reputed to be one of the most beautiful in the world, was a visit we both looked forward to. It provided an extra incentive.

The new approach to training I intended to adopt in Cape Town was to make use of some of the facilitators I had trained previously. I gave a good deal of thought to how I would use the new facilitators. Their training had taken them beyond the role of evaluators and had introduced them to the techniques of the trainer. I had produced a booklet to help them in their task, but I had some concerns as to how well the process would work.

My approach for the week's training was to make the plenary presentations to all the trainee supervisors myself, and then to hand over the group work to the facilitators. Their job would be to guide the groups, provide advice where needed and add any further information on the policy and framework for whole-school evaluation they felt the trainees needed. Once I had made the presentations, I intended to observe each group and monitor the effectiveness, not only of the group members, but also of the facilitators. I wanted to be sure that they had the skills to be able to carry forward the training for whole-school evaluation once my contract came to an end.

In the main, everything went according to plan. The presentations went well and the trainees responded as encouragingly as they had done in other Provinces. As usual, they responded to my jokes and teased me about my accent. In fact, one of the funniest of the stories I often tell was born here in Cape Town. One of the white participants came up to me on the second day and said, 'I hope you don't mind me saying this, but I know where you're from.'

'Of course you do,' I replied. 'I'm from England.'

'No, I know better than that. My son-in-law is from England and he is visiting. I went home last night and imitated your accent. He said immediately, 'It's obvious. He's from Barnsley.''

I looked at the lady with astonishment, wondering how a South African could imitate my accent so effectively as to enable her son-in-law to pinpoint the town near where I was born. I had been born about seven miles from Barnsley! It was the same village in which Geoffrey Boycott, the Yorkshire and England cricketer, had been born and perhaps, now that he was a cricket commentator, his accent had given her son-in-law a clue. But then, who would know Geoff was born in the same house as my father in the small mining village of Fitzwilliam, seven miles from Barnsley, and went to the same grammar school as I did?

As for the course, it seemed to go well and the facilitators did their job, other than for one group and one facilitator. The group was lively and challenging. Not surprisingly, part way through the first day the group members began to become frustrated by the apparent lack of knowledge of their facilitator. As I stood and observed, it was clear he had not done his homework and was unable to answer some of the important questions about whole-school evaluation they were asking. For instance, they were unsure how to make judgements on the range of resources a school had and how to report any shortcomings they thought were present. The facilitator stumbled through a sort of an answer, mentioning the need for sufficient dustbins for rubbish and the presence of sufficient cleaners, both of which are important, but neither, in light of what I had been teaching, crucial in moving forward learning in many of the country's schools. He never raised the real issues which concerned the shortage of trained staff, insufficient text books and exercise books for the children and the lack of technology for the teachers.

There was only one thing to do. I had a word with Linda and together we decided I should sit with the group and the facilitator should be asked to watch and learn. It was a delicate situation, but one which was well handled by the Province and, to the relief of the group members, they began to receive the sort of input they were seeking.

In the meantime, I discussed with the facilitator how he could improve his contribution and help the group understand more clearly the issues on which they were expected to report. To his credit, he took in what was said and he was able to take over supervision of the group again later in the week. For the last couple of days of the course he was able to help its members benefit from the training the course had to offer.

A very encouraging sign that school evaluation was beginning to impact were the five admirably presented training booklets provided for the course members by

Western Cape Province. In addition, they issued a booklet entitled '*Module for School Self-evaluation*'. It was a guide for schools to help them use self-evaluation to improve the quality of teaching and learning, to enable them to see the advantages of embedding the techniques of the self-evaluation system into quality assurance, and to help schools make use of attainment evidence when devising their school development plans. It successfully linked a school's vision to its development plan and the evaluation of the school's success in relation to that plan.

Another important element in the booklet was a framework for quality which included the district, Provincial and National authorities. The booklet went on to provide a series of questions designed to alert those involved in education to some of the critical areas which would need to be developed if a school was to provide the sort of education visualised in the national education policy.

The booklet was designed to help schools carry out self-evaluation rather than to help supervisors carry out external whole-school evaluations. Consequently, it was not used in the course, but the series of booklets gave clear indications of the encouraging progress being made in Western Cape, the Province which had been so hesitant at the start of the process of whole-school evaluation.

As luck would have it, there was a weekend of grace before I needed to make the journey for the next commitment Todd had planned for me before he had been taken ill. It gave me the opportunity to go to the

Newlands Cricket Ground and see the last day of a Test Match between South Africa and the West Indies. I had seen a sign to Newlands several times as I passed through Cape Town and now was a chance to follow it. When I suggested to Aurora that we should take the opportunity to go I could see she was overwhelmed with expectation. It took more than a suggestion to persuade her she might find it interesting! For me, to see the likes of Brian Lara in full flow was an occasion I didn't want to miss and so it was two people with two different emotions who approached the entrance gate.

We entered a ground which has been described by a man who obviously loved his cricket and had had the opportunity to make the visit we were now making, Reverend Christopher Chilvers, Canon Chancellor of Blackburn Cathedral, in the following words: '...*nothing beats a Test match played at Newlands, beneath one of the most spectacular mountains in the world. Furthermore, watching a game here provides a perfect setting for understanding deeper things about life, for ...aesthetics – as the Ancient Greeks knew only too well – sets the stage for contests which are often of the most epic proportion.*'

Well, I'm afraid what I saw that day was not of epic proportion. It was the last day of a match ending in a draw. But I did see the best of the South Africans and their attempts to prevent Brian Lara making a substantial number of runs. But there is little doubt that the setting of the ground, with Table Mountain its backdrop, is beautiful, and beautiful enough to get a 'Wow' from Aurora as we took our seats. Thereafter, while I watched, enjoyed the cricket and took the occasional photograph, Aurora spent the day enjoying a book written by her favourite writer, the South African J. M. Coetzee, who also had some interesting things to say about Cape Town and its area. Such is the differing impact of being in a *'perfect setting for understanding deeper things about life.'*

Chapter 11

The Passing of Todd Masilela

Once the course in Western Province was completed the arrangement was for me to travel back to KwaZulu-Natal to finish the final leg of the training in whole-school evaluation.

When Aurora and I left Cape Town we flew to Johannesburg and then were taken by car to Pretoria. I had heard further disturbing news of Todd's health whilst in Cape Town and decided to visit him again before moving on to KwaZulu-Natal. I learned he was now at home rather than in hospital and so went to the rather smart estate on which he lived. Although Todd was never able to afford the Mercedes his immediate superiors, black and white, seemed to be blessed with, he had managed to secure for his family a quality home.

I didn't know what to expect when I arrived to see him. His wife met me with the words, 'I'm afraid he's not very well.' She could not have understated Todd's condition any better. Her sad face and the quietness with which her children greeted me indicated the worst. When I went into his room, I saw a man with glazed eyes and an incredibly pale face; a man who didn't seem to recognise anybody, even his wife. He had no idea who I was and whatever attempts his wife made to draw his attention to me resulted only in the vacant movement of his head, a movement which failed to give any semblance of recognition. I uttered a few words, hoping to make some sort of contact, but it was pointless. I looked at Todd's wife and, without saying anything out loud, we seemed to agree it would be better if we left. I spent a little time with Todd's wife and children, offering what sympathy I could, but left a very sad man. My work with Todd had been fulfilling for both of us and through his efforts a great deal had been achieved in the attempts to indicate what was required if the principles behind Tirisano were to be realised. But I feared, as a result of what I saw on my visit, he would not live to see the benefits. I was right. By the time I reached KwaZulu-Natal, Todd had passed away.

In readiness for my work in KwaZulu-Natal, Todd, despite his illness and committed to the last, had sent out invitations to all the Provinces drawing their attention to the course, and inviting them to send anyone to Durban who wished to be trained as a supervisor. At the same time, he advised the Provinces they would be responsible for arranging and financing travel and accommodation. Todd was hoping that the invitation would enable Provinces throughout South Africa to send those they wished to be trained as supervisors and so fill any gaps in their provision for evaluating schools.

In addition, he had reminded Provinces they needed to send in any reports they had of the evaluations they had already carried out so that I could, in discussion with two report writers from each Province, test the credibility of the reports and help the two supervisors I was to work with produce a Provincial report. He was keen that any future annual reports would be based on valid Provincial reports and believed a session the two Provincial writers had with me would help towards that. He had drawn up a schedule of meetings before the worst of his illness, which meant I had meetings with representatives of Gauteng and the Free State on the first day, the North West Cape and KwaZulu-Natal on the following day, and Eastern Cape and Limpopo on the final day of consultations.

I found the meetings of great interest. They allowed me to ask questions of those who had carried out evaluations and to explore with them in detail how different Provinces supported their schools when they learned of the findings of the evaluations. It also gave me an insight into how the supervisors reported on the degree to which the quality of education in the different types of schools differed and the extent to which those differences were being tackled by the Provincial districts. Above all, the personal interviews gave me the opportunity to ask searching questions and verify or otherwise statements which were contained in the reports. It came as no surprise that the interviews revealed the reports, school and Provincial, from different Provinces were of variable quality and there was still a need for further training to ensure supervisors collected relevant information and presented it in a uniform way.

The head-to-head consultations in KwaZulu-Natal were planned for the beginning of the month. The middle of the month was set aside for me to make more visits, with appropriate personnel, to schools in several different Provinces, and during the last part of the month I was to run the final course on whole-school evaluation for the new supervisors in KwaZulu Natal.

I recognised the approach to whole-school evaluation within South Africa and my involvement with it would be seriously affected by Todd's death. The move out of education to another Government department by Dr Mgijima was to have further implications, but in no way as fundamental as those resulting from Todd's death. He had been the most significant player in the whole process, taking initiative when it was required, ensuring that Provincial officers were kept abreast of any developments as often as needed, but always seeing commitment to the principles espoused by the National Department of Quality Assurance as providing the route which would lead South Africa to Tirisano. It was Todd who communicated with me when I was in England and who provided most support for me when I was in South Africa.

When I think of what he did during the struggle for freedom and in the years later in his efforts to make that struggle worthwhile, I can't help but recognise a man strongly committed to the worthwhile cause of black equality. It gives me pleasure, and I'm sure it would do the same for him, that when I feed whole-school evaluation into the internet, even in 2015, reference to work in line with the policy being carried out in different

Provinces appears. Much of it is in the shape of research work carried out from different universities, but not all. To what extent the conclusions of the researchers are in line with what Todd and I worked so hard to achieve is difficult to say, but what I know of paper, it rarely bears the imprint of the efforts of those whose work it portrays.

In Limpopo, for example, a small number of primary schools which had been subject to whole-school evaluation produced research findings in 2009 which may well have been forecast, simply because of the time it takes significant change to occur. In England, schools have had to face up to a whole range of changes, especially because of the way Ofsted seems to operate, but most have led to relatively minor adjustments to an education system which has been responding to change since the end of the nineteenth century. In South Africa, whole-school evaluation and Tirisano were seeking fundamental change in a grossly unfair education system over a very much shorter period. It is not surprising, therefore, that in a little over eight years, the revolution Todd and his fellow countrymen were looking for had not occurred.

The earlier pilots of 2001 and the subsequent report published by the National Directorate identified many of the problems which have been identified in subsequent research. The 2001 report made clear that the national and provincial bodies were providing too little support to enable schools to overcome the limitations identified by the supervisors, a factor identified in later research. The outcome of this too limited support was that schools experienced difficulties in conducting their own evaluations, teachers' professional development was stunted because of the need for a greater input of resources, and external evaluation did not always work as effectively as it should in progressing educational provision.

Todd may well have been disappointed by these research findings, which suggested the weaknesses in some of the key areas of education seemed to have made little improvement, because these were matters which had also been recognised through the monitored evaluations of schools in his time, and represented issues which he had drawn attention to in his report on the pilot evaluations of 2001. There was nothing new in these later findings when they recognised that the state and the Provinces could do much more to address the known failures which were preventing South Africa from moving towards providing equal opportunities for all children in education, and fulfilling the aims outlined in Tirisano.

I have to admit, the research findings have come as no great surprise to me. I am not surprised that all the work the National Directorate had done as a result of Todd's promptings has yet to produce the outcomes he had hoped for. We both knew it would take time and probably far more than half a dozen years or so after the introduction of whole-school evaluation. I had been involved with school inspection in England and elsewhere for too long to believe in miracles!

But I'm sure Todd would have been pleased in the way the research confirmed there was a need for the state to have a clear strategy and to pursue it with consistency and determination if the aims he sought were to be achieved. I'm also sure he would have been pleased to read an excerpt from the News Letter of the Western Cape, published in 2007, in which Linda Rose, who was by then Director of Quality Assurance in the Province, stated the Province's intention to address the findings of the education department's latest evaluations of selected schools in the Province. She asserted it was the Province's intention to continue to carry out whole-school evaluations because they were part of the national system and covered the nine areas crucial to achieving a successful education for all children.

The evaluations which had been carried out in 2007 in the 27 schools in Western Cape identified one of the over-riding issues noted in the pilots of 2002 and later in Limpopo. They concerned what was, in the framework for whole-school evaluation, implied by focus area four – the need for Provinces to ensure continuous professional training for school leaders and staff. It was, Linda Rose promised, the Provincial department's intention to provide circuit teams and educational specialists in all the district offices of Western Cape to ensure that schools in every area had appropriate support as they endeavoured to write their own specific improvement plans based on school evaluations, whether internal or external, and meet the objectives they set.

As my experience with Ofsted has taught me, change is an imperative in any system of school inspection; the policy for whole-school evaluation has been, in all probability, amended over the years since its introduction in 2001. Nevertheless, I live in the hope that the underlying principles designed to improve the education of every child in South Africa, whether black or white, which were so dear to the National Directorate and those committed to whole-school evaluation, have been maintained.

Chapter 12

The Other South Africa

With the last session of the training in KwaZulu-Natal my three to four year contract in South Africa came to an end. I can't really remember how I felt. I had become so attached to the country and the people I met I suspect I was sad to leave, but I know I was determined to return, no matter in what capacity. As it was, Aurora felt much the same. It was no surprise, therefore, that when we were back in England we began, almost immediately, to plan a holiday in South Africa.

We had no idea where we might go but the internet came, as it so often does, to our rescue. Aurora fed in 'holiday properties for rent in South Africa' and up came Bayview Heights. It was an ideal looking flat with two bedrooms and in a position overlooking False Bay, just south of Cape Town and in a former British naval base, Simons Town. As it happened, the flat was owned by a young couple, the wife being of Italian origin. Once Aurora had made contact, the relationship worked to the advantage of both; Ginevra found someone with whom she could converse in Italian and Aurora found us an ideal flat for a holiday. All the transactions were made and shortly after Christmas, our winter and South Africa's summer, we were on our first visit to South Africa as genuine tourists. South Africa became a different experience.

After some discussion, we decided to drive from Johannesburg to Cape Town. Now that we were not pressed by the commitments of work we wanted to see as much of South Africa as we could. A drive through the centre of the country from Johannesburg to Cape Town offered us the perfect opportunity.

I hired a car at the airport in Johannesburg and then drove through the city towards the N1 motorway. The route we followed took us south towards Bloemfontein and well east of Kimberley, two cities which I had already visited on my travels. Instead of journeying into Bloemfontein, we cut off the high way and made our way to a small self-contained property we had rented for the night just east of the city.

Having parked the car we approached what we saw as a mainly wooden lodge, but before we could get through the door we were welcomed by two fine looking peacocks which were wandering around the small garden. They were friendly enough, though didn't allow us to get too close, or should I say we didn't allow them to get too close. I had never been so near to peacocks before and was not sure how they reacted to humans, but the experience seemed to be enjoyed by both of us, Aurora and me as well as the two peacocks. We were treated to a display of a colourful tail by what we took to be the male before we managed to get our things inside the lodge and organise ourselves for our one night stay.

A little later in the evening we decided to go into Bloemfontein, primarily for a meal, but also to see the Parliament Buildings and the Court of Justice. Having taken the easy way out by having a pizza in one of the many restaurants along the high street, we walked for a while down streets which contained the museum, the usual memorials to the Boers before returning to our lodge to settle in for a restful night after what had been a tiring day's driving. We had seen some significant buildings in Bloemfontein but recognised we had given ourselves insufficient time to properly experience what it had to offer.

Next morning when we rose to leave, we realised we were actually on the edge of a game park. In the distance and through fynbos we could see a variety of wild animals, impala and kudu, wandering around within what was a typically beautiful African setting. It was tempting to stay longer and enjoy the sights, but we knew we had a long journey ahead and so we were on our way in good time. Certainly, it was sometime before, or it seemed to be, the peacocks had begun their daily patrol of the garden.

Our immediate destination was the small town Aurora had identified, and one we had never visited, called Graaf Reinet. In order to reach it we had to leave the N1 and take a road through some gloriously attractive countryside, laced with the wide range of vegetation we had grown used to during our visits to South Africa.

We had booked to stay for a couple of nights in Graaf Reinet, a small town which we came to recognise as one of the most beautiful we had visited. Its well-tended gardens, wide streets and well-maintained houses and churches, especially the magnificent Victorian Gothic Dutch Reformed church in its centre, represented much of what white South Africa had enjoyed during apartheid. But what became of particular interest to me was the Coldstream Guards' Club. Having done my military service in the Welsh Guards it came as a fascinating surprise that the Coldstreams, with whom I had marched side-by-side on many public occasions, should have left their mark in what seemed such a distant place. It was only when I sat drinking coffee and eating some wonderful, freshly baked scones that I began to relate their presence to the Boer War and so find part of the explanation. The coffee, scones, the club, the Coldstreams, Graaf Reinet, and the Boer War have been related in my mind since that day. As for Aurora, she was so taken with the scones that she asked for the recipe. The chef in the Guard's club was delighted to pass it on. It has remained fixed to our kitchen wall ever since and encourages Aurora to bake the most delightful scones each time we have visitors.

We found the pleasant guest house in which we were to stay along one of the attractive streets branching off the high street. The owners made us very welcome and I suspect we were something of a treasure, being English and so far from our homeland.

Unfortunately, it was here, for some reason, I suffered another severe attack of trigeminal neuralgia. It was a problem I had had for several years and for reasons seemingly unknown to doctors it could attack at any time. This was one of them. It may have been the result of the tiring six-hundred or so miles journey we had made that day, but my experience with the condition told me there could be other factors which were responsible. As a reader, you need to talk with others who suffer from the same problem if you are looking for an explanation. I'm afraid I cannot offer one. The severity of the pain made me wonder if I was going to be able to drive the rest of the way to Cape Town, but fortunately it eased overnight.

Before we left Graaf Reinet, Aurora took the opportunity to ask questions of the owner, starting with her usual, 'Can I ask a question?' My stomach fluttered for a moment as I wondered what the question was likely to be and whether there was any likelihood of it upsetting our hosts. Then she went on, 'How do the farmers manage to have such large farms? In my country it is normal for land to be divided among the children when their parents die. I would have thought there would be lots of smaller farms.' The response she received from our embarrassed-looking host was, 'They've no problem. They've always gone and simply grabbed more land if they've needed it.' It was enough to satisfy Aurora, whose views about what she saw as capitalists and their desire to own more and more seemed to be confirmed.

Another question was to the landlady. Aurora asked if she knew anywhere else we could stay on our way to Cape Town. 'I have a friend who has a guest house in Mossel Bay. It's a lovely guest house and I have no problem in recommending it. In fact, I was only talking to her this morning. She told me she has a room spare, which overlooks the Bay. If you'd like it, I'll ring her back.' For once, a question of Aurora's hadn't caused any embarrassment and when we said we would like to take the room our hostess went to talk again with her friend and let her know we would like to stay. And so Mossel Bay became our destination for the day.

We set off on the next part of our journey, another four hundred plus miles, in good heart. Despite the distance we had to travel we were tempted into an exploration of the area around Graaf Reinet and a section of South Africa's semi-arid desert, the Karoo. This eventually brought us to a high point in the surrounding mountains which was called the Valley of Desolation. I had difficulty understanding the name, and still do, because, as far as I could see, it was not really a valley but a series of high rocks left as a result of volcanic erosion over many years – or at least, that is what I understood it to be. We could see from here the enormous flat plane known as the Great Karoo, through part of which we were to journey. We could also see the two shanty towns on the outskirts of Graaf Reinet; the square, untidy blocks which seemed to be present around many of the most beautiful towns in South Africa. Once more they underlined the huge differences in the lifestyles of blacks and whites even after the release and Presidency of Mandela. They provided further proof there was still much to do if the equalities of Tirisano were to be achieved.

As we approached the steep and narrow roadway which led us up to the top of the Valley of Desolation we saw more of South Africa's many species of animals, the Kudu, Blesbuck, Springbuck and Mountain Rhebuck, dashing away from the car into the bush – no doubt they saw all cars as prospective enemies. We also saw several blue cranes feeding in one of the large open fields so common throughout South Africa. It was a sight which encouraged us to stop so that we could get a much better view of the attractive birds we had never seen before.

Eventually, we left the mountains and began to cross the plain. Aurora took over the driving to give me some rest as we travelled along the straight roads of the plain. The glorious mountains provided a superb backdrop. We saw no one and no other cars. We were almost coming to believe that the land was uninhabited. Occasionally, we passed a farmhouse away in the distance and marvelled at the amount of land the farmer seemed to control. After the long, but fantastic drive during which we explored what was to us a new and beautiful land, seemingly untouched by civilisation, we arrived early enough in Mossel Bay to be able to have a walk round the Bay and get the feel of a town which was one of the few which didn't inspire us. It seemed to be from another generation when compared to the town we had left that morning, Graaf Reinet. Modern, and what to us were uninteresting buildings, surrounded a very ordinary beach which bore few of the attractions of Durban. However, we did have a lovely room, with windows overlooking the Bay, which appeared much more enticing as the evening lights came on.

Next morning we had an early breakfast, knowing we had another long journey. We were keen to see Cape

Town again and hoped Simons Town was as attractive a place as the internet had suggested.

Our journey took us along part of the road we had travelled some months earlier as we were reaching the end of the Garden Route. The sight of Table Mountain with its tablecloth-covering of cloud first thing in the morning and the peaks of the Twelve Apostles providing a backdrop to Camps Bay lives in the memory long after a visit. Those stately mountains are in stark contrast to the shanty towns with their poorly repaired wooden shacks and rubbish, places of habitation which were so different to those houses we had seen in Graaf Reinet. It is not easy to dispel images of the conditions in which many Africans still lived.

Cape Town certainly deserves its reputation as one of the most beautiful cities in the world. It is a city we were destined to visit several more times in future years as we were drawn back to a country with which we had fallen in love. That desire to re-visit was cemented by our holiday that year. The flat we had rented had an ideal location. Although on an estate of similar flats, it was very quiet and had a very private terrace. It was positioned on the edge of the estate and at a height which gave us a fantastic view of False Bay. We could sit on the terrace for breakfast, lunch or tea in December and January, those horribly cold and sometimes snowy months in England, and drink morning coffee whilst overlooking the sea.

We had a first-rate view of ships entering and leaving Simons Town harbour, which was now a base for the South African navy, and the many small yachts which looked like small white swans as they passed to and fro in the distance. The presence of smartly uniformed men walking along the streets gave us confidence as we moved around the town's busy streets or went into one of the many restaurants for a meal. For once, nobody warned us of dangers lurking behind the corners and our experience confirmed there was no need.

Chapter 13

The Cape of Good Hope

Western Province is an unbelievable place to visit. The innumerable places which are worth going to, in and around Cape Town, the capital, leave the mind confused as to where to start. This is certainly true as I seek to write about how we spent our time once my contract had terminated and we had returned on holiday. As I have said earlier in the story, we intended to spend more free time than we had been allowed when I was leading courses so that we could savour a country we felt privileged to be able to visit.

It's amazing how the history I learned in school re-emerges as I travel to different places – the prison colony of Hobart as I travelled through Tasmania, the graves of war heroes associated with my journeys through France and Germany, the American Civil War on my visits to the USA and the importance of the Suez Canal when I travelled to Egypt. It seemed as though the influence of my history teachers would be with me forever. It was the same on our visits to South Africa. I could not escape what I had learned about the Boer Wars, about the warlike propensities of the Zulu, or about the significance in history of The Cape of Good Hope and the founding of Cape Town.

I had learned about the Dutch East India Company and how its merchantmen had developed the port in Table Bay as an assist as they rounded the southern tip of Africa on their way to India and the Far East. The Cape, we were taught, presented the sailing ships of those earlier days with the roughest seas to navigate of all the southern capes. But apparently, that was not always the case – much depended on the conditions which prevailed when the ships rounded the Cape. Bartholomew Dias was reputed to have called it 'The Cape of Storms', while for Sir Francis Drake it was 'The fairest Cape in all the world', and for King John II of Portugal, who, I assume, never sailed around the Cape, it was 'The Cape of Good Hope,' because it opened up the sea route to the wealth of the East.

What is more certain is what we were taught about how the English sailors had taken over the trading station which the Dutch had founded and, dare I say it, learned with some pride how the British Government eventually annexed the whole peninsula, introduced British law and forced the Boers to make the Great Trek. Its history meant the Cape peninsular was a place to visit and the proximity of Simons Town, located mid-way between Cape Town and Cape Point, provided us with the ideal opportunity.

I remember, when we first made our way to the Cape, how the images of storms and rough seas coloured my mind. I ought to have known better. The days we spent looking across False Bay, named because it had been wrongly thought to lead to the East by the earliest explorers, should have given a clue. It was, not surprisingly, usually calm and placid during the weeks over Christmas and New Year when we stayed in Simon's Town gazing across to the mountains which overlooked Hermanus, a town famous for whale watching, and thinking of our fellow Brits in the cold and dark of mid-winter.

We didn't know what to expect when we made our first visit to the Cape of Good Hope. In some ways we were like the first explorers, eager to discover. The road we took went through the main street of the well-appointed Simon's Town which, as usual with South African towns, had its neighbouring shanty town. We followed the line of the central mountains on the one side and the Ocean on the other. The road led us past The Boulders, where we stopped to see the jackass penguins pit-patting their rather ungainly way across the sand and then weave through the shallow inlet with torpedo-like grace. It was fascinating to watch them at a time which seemed to be one for creating relationships. Many were in pairs and some had their young nestling close to their chests, but others, seeming to have failed to gain a partner, were wandering aimlessly first in one direction and then in another in their efforts to find one. Whether they were successful or not wasn't our concern and so having satisfied our curiosity we took to the road again.

The road took us around Partridges' Corner and up to the gate which led into the Cape of Good Hope nature reserve. The first wildlife we saw was the long-legged ostriches and, scurrying in and around the rocks, what we came to know as rock hyrax and dassie. We heeded the warnings about baboons when they appeared, though it's fair to say not everybody did. I found it difficult to understand how people could take the risk of lowering the car window to throw out food when the warnings were so clear.

I kept the car moving along the surprisingly long drive through the nature reserve, captivating because of it flora and fauna. We had seen lots of fynbos in other parts of Western Cape but here it was wild and unspoiled. There were lots of proteas in the bush land and not surprisingly lots of birds such as sugar birds and sand birds which were attracted to the flowers. The sight of more of the long-legged ostriches, living in the wild, brought back memories of those in cages in Oudtshoorn and led to our discussing whether or not these ostriches had been born in the wild or had escaped from an ostrich farm.

We spotted more animals grazing, the bontebok and red heartbeest, as well as the odd tortoise as it crawled slowly across the road, and a wide range of different insects. It was fascinating. And then out to sea, way in the distance, we became excited by what we thought we might be seeing. A spout of water suddenly shot into the air. We screwed our eyes in an effort to see the whale which we hoped was responsible. But we were never able to get the sighting which would have confirmed or otherwise what was responsible. 'We saw a whale,' was a story we could tell but not with the conviction we would have liked. What we could talk about with certainty, however, was the shoal of dolphins we saw later that day as they bounced, sometimes one after another and sometime in unison, through the waves. We were climbing our way from the car park along the path and up the steps to the famous lighthouse when they appeared and processed through the blue waters to the delight of everyone who was lucky enough to see them.

The most persistent animals were the baboons, adults and babies. They commanded the sides of the road and on occasions would sit in the middle, forcing us to slow and hope they would move on. Fortunately, we didn't get into any sort of conflict with them as we drove up to the car park where we saw lots more. The car park seemed swallowed up with baboons as they moved between, under and over cars, seemingly impervious to the shouts of owners, always looking for something to eat and, unfortunately, finding it as some car owners seemed to enjoy throwing them food despite all the warnings.

I found a quiet corner in which to park the car, hopeful that it would avoid the attention of the baboons. All I could do was hope. From the car park we climbed the steps, pausing to enjoy the superb views of rocks, beaches and seas until we reached the terraces which had been built, clearly for that purpose, around the old lighthouse. With the intention of reaching the new lighthouse we decided to follow the fairly narrow path which led in that direction. It was flanked by a steep drop into the sea and had to be taken with care, especially in the wind which was blowing that day. As we moved along the path, we had to hold on to the surrounding wooden rail to make sure we crossed safely. The tricky bit would have been if other visitors had needed to pass us as they made their way back. Our good fortune on that day was we seemed to be the only ones braving the wind. We moved around the Point to a position from which we could look down on to the new lighthouse which was on the furthermost rocks and realised there was no way we could reach it; we could approach the old lighthouse with ease, but not the new one. Its rocky position at the end of the Point meant we could not explore it in the same way we had explored the old lighthouse and so we could do no more than look down at it from a distance and then begin our return.

We had decided a coffee would be a better option than trying to scale the rocks and returned to the cafe by the car park. Here, we ordered coffee and scones, not ones of the quality of those from the Coldstream Club in Graaff Reinet, but ones we thought would be enjoyable enough. The cafe was fairly busy but we found seats, placed the coffee and scones on the table and settled to chat about the spectacular sights we had seen that day. It was as I reached across the table for my scone that a huge hairy arm suddenly appeared. It beat me to the scone. As I looked up in shock, I saw the arm belonged to a large baboon. It was hanging on to a branch just by the side of the cafe and had seen its chance. It was obviously used to getting its food that way and had seized its opportunity. It probably knew it was a more than startled Englishman it was stealing from.

To my delight, it clearly had difficulty getting rid of the wrapping around the scone. To solve the problem, it simply put the whole lot into its mouth, chewed and swallowed. I decided, in the circumstances, a coffee was enough and Aurora came to the same conclusion, feeling it safer to leave her scone on the plate so that the baboon could have a second helping if it wanted one. The last thing either of us wanted was a fight with a big, hairy baboon.

On another one of our visits to Cape Point we walked along the path which, on our first, we had thought might take us to the new lighthouse. Our previous experience told us it didn't, but our walk along the path was not in vain. We saw, just below us, what was an attractive sandy bay. We decided to go down and explore. The descent was a little tricky, but the path we followed took us right onto the lovely, crisp sand from where we could see beautiful vegetation between the rocks, rolling waves and hundreds of seals sunning themselves wherever they could. The cape orchids were in full bloom and clusters of other attractive, exotic flowers, as well as providing a lovely scent for Aurora, provided whatever the tiny sun birds were looking for as they darted from one delicate petal to another. We spent some time on the beach, watching the birds, the seals and taking in the wider sights, allowing the warmth to penetrate, before clambering back up to the path and eventually the car park. Our normal return route when we visited Cape Point was to follow the westerly coastline towards a village I could never resist visiting. How could I? I had spent many days during my holidays in Britain in Bridlington and neighbouring Scarborough. Here, in South Africa, was a village with the magic name, Scarborough. But there the similarity ended. How a village with such different sea, sand and weather could end up with the same name as a holiday resort open to the winds of the North Sea was baffling, but it had to be visited. Just to wander along the beach in the calm warmth of a sunny day would bring back different memories, memories of waves battering against sea walls, dampening everyone who went too close, and only the brave being tempted into the water for a swim.

After savouring the shopping in a different Scarborough, a South African Scarborough protected from any Easterly winds by the slopes of Slangkop and Red Hill, rather than open to those cold blustery North Sea breezes as was the case in the Yorkshire Scarborough, we would continue along the coast to Kommetjie, a beach which was very popular with those who looked to surf the waves. There were things about the Kommetjie area of the Atlantic coast which were reminiscent of the Yorkshire East coast, its wind and waves especially, but neither detracted from the southern sunshine.

When we had seen enough of the Atlantic and the coast it washed against, always wary of coming across any of the sharks the many warnings cautioned about, we would cross over to Glencairn and then on to our flat in Simons Town, where we could sit on the terrace and view the naval harbour, with its comings and goings.

Aurora and I used to sit with our coffee ostensibly chatting, but I could not rid myself of the question, *'Why did my ancestors, long ago, choose to live in a cold and rainy West of Ireland rather than a country similar to this, the sunny, balmy South Africa?'* I will never know

189

the answer, but many an Irishman will tell me they knew exactly what they were doing. The same Irishman may also be able to tell me who was the first to sail around the Cape of Good Hope and open up the trade route to the East. Had he journeyed up and down the Cape as much as we did he would have seen the statue of Dias on the Western Coast and the high cross dedicated to Da Gama on the Eastern Coast. The former made the first journey around the tip but had to return because of rough seas and lack of provisions, whilst the latter used the passage around the Cape to make his memorable round the world voyage.

We had read that Cape Town was a beautiful city and there was very little about it which disappointed us. However, we were unable to escape the worst of its past, the days of apartheid. As usual, the receptionist in the hotel in which I had stayed previously when I was working in Cape Town had warned me about which streets and areas to avoid. Now, a tourist with Aurora at my side, I knew which areas to avoid, but also knew there was enough of beauty in Cape Town to make it well worth a visit. I decided to drive from Simons Town through Fishoek, Miuzenberg and along the main road to the city. We also passed through the very wealthy wine-growing areas of Tokai and Constantia with their beautiful trees, high walls and unmistakable warning signs, '*Armed Response*'.

Like all cities, Cape Town is busy with vehicles of all types, either moving along the streets or parked in the most unusual places. When we visited, our first problem, usually, was to find somewhere to park. On the occasion about which I am writing we were in luck. Just beyond the busy market stalls and the City Hall I found a car park. Our first real tour of Cape Town was about to begin.

Or I thought it was. I'd forgotten about the market. It was Aurora's first stop. She was in among the stalls looking for something which would suit her taste and provide her with memories for the future. The choice was a locally made African skirt and dress, articles of clothing Aurora wears on occasions to this day. From the market we moved on through the streets and then, to our amazement, we came to the Jewish Museum. It was something we had not expected, though knowing what had happened to Jews over the years we should not have been surprised.

The synagogue in which it was housed was the oldest in South Africa and reflected the long and influential association the Jewish people have had with the country. Once inside, we watched audio visual presentations and examined artefacts which brought together the old and the new about a community and its relationships with a country which offered some sort of refuge from the persecution suffered by Jews in Eastern Europe and elsewhere.

In part of the city nearby, District Six, we found the museum dedicated to the black and coloured citizens who had been driven from their homes in the area as part of a planned clearance during the time of apartheid. Here, there were sign posts bearing street names which no longer existed and lists of the names of families which had disappeared, vivid reminders of how those who had lived in District Six had been treated. Fortunately, we could see that things were slowly beginning to change, even in the townships, a result of Mandela's interest in the fate of his fellow countrymen.

As we came to know Cape Town, we realised it had much to say about the South Africa of the past. Not only in its museums and the surrounding shanty towns but in the buildings which graced different parts of the city; The Castle of Good Hope where the military forces of the British were once stationed and which is now also a museum dedicated to the military, and the impressive town hall which stands opposite. A walk we made through a well-kept garden, its lawns manicured and its centre-pieces thick with blooms of different types, brought us to the front of the government buildings, not quite as impressive to us as those in Pretoria but which had an attraction which signified their importance as a centre of Government.

It was on another visit we took the route which took us by the Lions Head, a peak which we had seen from the city. The road led us up behind our flat in Bay View, past Admiral's Kloof, the grave of the naval dog Nuisance Justin, the well signposted Silver Mines and to a point where we stopped and could look down upon Cape Town, its fine buildings, its harbour, its sandy bay and the blue sea which washed the city's shores. It is a fine city, and as I have already said, it is rated as one of the ten most beautiful in the world. But as we viewed from on high we were left wondering how one comes to such a judgement. We were looking at a city which had seen colonial countries fight over it; a city which had seen its black and coloured populations maltreated by white, Dutch settlers; a city from which the same people had been driven beyond its borders by white supremacists; and now a city to which tourists flocked to see how proudly it wished to show its history. Were Aurora and I being drawn into believing that such a history was inevitable and to forget that desire, hatred and lust had had much to do with what we were looking at?

No matter, we fell into the trap. We took the city and its surrounds for what they were, and accepted that some have much and some have little. As we sat for a moment and drifted into talking about South Africa's past and prospects for the future, we recognised we were not in a position to make judgements about the past, and perhaps we hoped we never would be.

We decided to move on from our spot overlooking Cape Town and then noticed a good deal of activity on Signal Hill. I looked at my watch and realised noon was approaching. It was time for the firing of the cannon, a tradition dating back to the eighteenth century. A short detour took us within sight of the military as they marched onto the small square, raised the flag and prepared for the firing of the midday cannon. At twelve o'clock precisely, the cannon sent its daily signal across the city.

On this particular day, we had decided to visit another significant area of Cape Town, the Victoria and Alfred Waterfront. We had already enjoyed the vast beach at Noordhoek, which seemed to be used more for horse riding than building sand castles and splashing about in the sea water, and travelled across Chapman's Peak to enjoy the fantastic views, especially the beaches surrounding the blue sea in Hout Bay. We had been to Cape Point, which was no longer a stranger to us, and we had visited several of the villages along the Cape Peninsular, including Scarborough. The Victoria and Alfred Waterfront had been quietly waiting on our list of places to see but there had been so many other things of interest that we had not yet visited it.

The Waterfront is fascinating. Wherever we looked there were people, or, if we looked downwards to the sea and between the wooden supports of the harbour, great hairy seals, some with babies, others simply sunning themselves. The seals seemed to epitomise what life might be like for those with no ambition other than to sleep. Most slept beneath the sun and only occasionally turned, seeming to want to make sure the sun reached every part of, what seemed to us, their huge bodies. They were undisturbed by the people or the music I could hear as we moved further into the harbour and absorbed more of what it had to offer.

There seemed to be a harmony with the music and the people, the shops and the restaurants. Nothing seemed out of place. Even the tree under which the small band of black musicians was playing the ever popular jazz songs was where we felt it should be and provided just enough shade for the musicians. It also offered protection from the hot sun to the small crowd which gathered to listen, before throwing their rand into the hat and moving on to the next source of entertainment, possibly a group of black dancers, singers or drummers.

The talent these groups displayed made me wonder where they had learned their skills and how they had coped in the country's worst times. We followed the pattern, but I lingered by the band, impressed by the trumpet player. I had been a cornet and trumpet player for as long as I can remember and played to a level which gained me a position in some of the best brass bands in England, as well as the Band of Her Majesty's Welsh Guards, but I had always found improvising on a tune difficult. I needed to be able to read the notes and then I could play. Here was a trumpet player to whom the skill of improvising seemed to come so easily that, without any music, he could lead the three or four other musicians through every piece with a lilt that was captivating. How I wished I could have done the same.

As we wandered around the rest of the Waterfront we were tempted into one of the two aquariums. We were to see, on another visit, a variety of fish in the fresh water of the Silver Mines, for example bass and carp, and we had already seen, in the seas around the Cape, dolphin and our assumed whale, but we needed to look into the great tanks of an aquarium to view what we had not yet been able to see, the fearsome shark. And the one we saw was fearsome. As we stood with others who had come to have a similar experience, a huge white fish swam up to the glass pane in which it was encased, peered at us, opened its mouth to show us its terrifying teeth and then, at a speed almost too quick to follow, turned and headed back into the depths of the tank. It was then we saw the whip of the tail and the fish's most distinctive feature, the pointed fin.

As we moved around the harbour we came across what for me was always a temptation – a coffee bar. There seemed to be coffee bars at almost every turn. But fortunately, there were other activities which took my interest. Various people, black, white and coloured, were displaying their different skills, from dancing in groups and singing in small choirs to seeking to sell what they had made or created – art, pottery, clothes and recorded music, usually of native African origin. Some were on stalls, some on cloth sheets laid out on the harbour floor and some were in shops, the windows of which we could not pass without spending some time studying what they had for sale. It was a tourist's paradise.

Chapter 14

Aurora

We completed our visit of the Waterfront by the end of the morning. We had had a fascinating experience wandering around an eye-catching area but by one o'clock we felt it time to move on. We returned to the car park and began to study the map which Aurora had left on her seat as we discussed how we should spend the rest of the day. 'We could go along the coastal road further north. I imagine it's an interesting drive,' I suggested. 'Isn't there a place called Table View people talk about? That'd be a good place to see the mountain from.'

'You feel you can do more driving and not get too tired?' Aurora asked, but I could tell from the tone of her voice she was as keen as I was to see what lay north of Cape Town. And so it was agreed. We got into the car, Aurora put the open map on her knees, and we set off. We followed the coastal road, enjoying more of South Africa's scenic beauties. When we reached Table View I found a spot to park which overlooked the bay and the seeming hundred or so surfers who were taking advantage of the wind and waves. We got out of the car, turned to our left and had a superb view of one of the most famous mountains in the world. It was awe-inspiring. Aurora had the camera out in no time and the click, click, click ensured we would have a record of that view of Table Mountain, which sought to please us by covering itself with a thin white cloud, the tablecloth, and of the surfers braving the Atlantic Ocean, for the rest of our lives.

Having absorbed the delights of Table View we moved on, first through Melbosstrand and then on to St Helena's Bay, the place where Vasco da Gama is said to have first set foot in South Africa in the fifteenth century. With its calm seas, yachts and impressive lighthouse, it became another place of special memories for us. From the Bay, Aurora used the map to guide me inland and away from the coast with the intention of our picking up the N7 and speeding our way back to Cape Town.

And then the most surprising thing! Without any warning from the detailed map on my guide's knee we saw a signpost turning off the main macadamised road down one which was no more than a rough track. It signalled Aurora! How could we resist the urge to go and visit a town or perhaps village with my wife's name? We bumped our way down the track beginning to think we had made a mistake and should turn back, but its narrowness meant it would have been as difficult as continuing.

Eventually, we found ourselves in the square of the quaint village, a village which didn't have the overlooked, busy streets of the old English villages I had learned about in history. There was nothing about it which resembled The Shambles in York or Pottergate in Lincoln. The houses we could see were spread around in spaces which seemed to have challenged any thought the villagers may have had of creating a main street and there was little which caught the eye other than the beautiful mountains within which the village was set, and the seasonal yellow, pink and orange flowers.

We could see little else other than what appeared to be a single shop and the several sandveld houses surrounding what we took to be the square, no doubt created to enable the villagers to come together on occasions of celebration, though what they were likely to celebrate was not particularly evident as we looked around. It was quiet; it was peaceful

For once, I had no problem parking, a difficulty I usually found in most towns I visited, whether it was in South Africa or elsewhere. We felt we had to get out of the car, walk and enjoy another Aurora, an Aurora which seemed to lack the heart of the one sitting beside me.

My wife Aurora, undaunted by the calm and quiet by which she was surrounded, decided to test out Western Cape humour by plucking up courage and going into the only shop we could see. Her opening gambit, 'Can I ask a question?' had my stomach tingling. What was she going to ask and would it result in us having to make a quick getaway? I had experience of this question and was to experience it later, in much more embarrassing circumstances. But on this occasion it was asked as an opening to a question which left the shopkeeper and me with no more than surprised looks on our faces. Showing her name by opening her passport, Aurora said, 'Because I've allowed you to name this lovely village after me, do I get a reduction on the price of a packet of biscuits?' I breathed a sigh of relief and wondered what harm there could be in such an inoffensive question. The look of surprise on the shopkeeper's face was eventually replaced with what I can only describe as a stiff smile and the response, 'Biscuits are five Rand a pack for everybody, Madam.' She peered even closer at Aurora and added, 'Despite their name.' Aurora looked at me as if seeking some sort of support before replying, 'I was intrigued by the name of the village and thought you might be interested in my name. As you can see,' Aurora said, attempting a friendlier smile than that of the shopkeeper, 'I meant it as a joke.'

It's fair to say that further attempts to open up a friendly discussion about the name Aurora were received with more interest. It's also fair to say that the price of the biscuits remained the same.

We had an even more interesting experience as we moved through the rest of the square and just beyond it. We came across a small stone monument of more significance than we at first realised. We walked up to it and around it as we sought to read the inscription. We discovered it recorded the first triangulated survey carried out by a scientist who was known by the name of the Abbe a de La Caille at that time but who is now known as Nicholas Louis. The inscription reads *'This is the site of the Maclear beacon positioned in 1838 near the original North terminal of the Arc of Meridian positioned by Abbe de la Caille, the first surveyor to introduce Geodetic Surveying into South Africa.'* It meant nothing to me, but obviously a great deal to the Abbe as he sought to determine the radius of the earth in the Southern Hemisphere by using triangulation between Cape Town, Darling and Aurora. He came to the conclusion the earth was flatter towards the South Pole than towards the North Pole, a theory later challenged and disproved. Even so, the monument to his work on the outskirts of Aurora has been declared a National Monument by the South African Government.

The day of surprises was not yet complete. Aurora was able to find a different route back to the N7, one which was macadamised and allowed us to reach the motorway without trouble. But again we were distracted by a road sign. This time we were not tempted to follow its direction. We simply laughed. The sign was directing us to 'The Tower of Pizza,' a wooden built cafe we could see just off the roadside. We never discovered whether the tower was leaning or not, but we wouldn't have been surprised if it were. Even so, we were pretty sure the pizza would have a wonderful taste and had we had time we may well have gone to enjoy its delights.

Chapter 15

Table Mountain

The following day, we decided to brave Table Mountain. We both knew Aurora was not good at heights but we thought she would be fine in the cable car and, hopefully, once we reached our destination she would find the summit flat and walkable. At least that's what it looked like from below.

We joined others in the cable car and headed skywards. In no time, Aurora was down, sitting on the floor, fearful of what she could see over the sides of the cable car. We managed it to the top but couldn't dispel from our minds the thought of the descent as we sought to enjoy the experience of one of the most famous mountains in the world.

As we left the cable car we were stunned by what we could see down below us. The views were magnificent. Cape Town, as beautiful as ever, seemed small enough to fit into the palm of my hand. It snuggled in its bay below the mountain and its two associates, Devil's Peak and Lion's Head, a strip of yellow separating the city from the blue ocean which seemed to stretch for ever. Today, the sea was calm and the white specks created by angry waves were nowhere to be seen. I took hold of Aurora's hand, pulled her closer and whispered in her ear, 'Worth the effort, my love?'

'Oh, yes,' she replied as she began to move around the small terrace which had been prepared for those who wished to sightsee before moving further onto the mountain top. Not surprisingly, we had not moved very far before the usual attractions surrounded us – temptations to sit and drink coffee, have a beer or buy a souvenir. A beer was the thing, and for both of us. I had found the journey, despite the odd slowing down and bumping no problem, but for Aurora it had been very stressful. She certainly needed a 'pick me up'. We sat and enjoyed our drink, listening to the 'Wows' and watching those who had already completed their exploration of the mountain top, chattering with the sort of enthusiasm only a trip of this sort could produce, as they boarded the cable car,

The expanse of the mountain top amazed me and I still don't know why. I had viewed it often enough from below and also from along the coast, and been impressed by its size. I had also seen the way the morning cloud settled on the summit as though it were a table cloth being prepared to offer breakfast. It is not surprising it was this feature which had led to someone giving the mountain its name.

We discovered we could walk a good distance either along flat areas or up and down clefts in the rock. In fact, we wandered so far away from the cable car station as to be almost out of sight of other tourists. We found an ideal place to sit and enjoy a sandwich Aurora had prepared before we left Simons Town. There was a breeze, but it was warm and in no way as threatening as the wind had been when we had been tempted, on one of our earlier journeys to South Africa, to try to cross the Sentinel, a mountain in the Drakensburgs. On that occasion, we had climbed to the path which led around and upwards, hoping to reach the summit, but we were driven back by the power of the wind and the threat of being driven off the path despite the handrail which had been put there so that such a fate could be avoided. Wisely, we had not tried to brave the elements and reach the top of the Sentinel without any sort of guidance. On a fine, clear day it may have been something worth doing, but on a wind-swept mountain covered in mist it would have been a very foolish venture.

On that day, we had taken the sensible option and returned to ground level. But today, we were at the summit, almost three-and-a half-thousand feet above sea level, of an even more famous mountain, and entirely safe. There was little wind, warm sunshine and superb views which we could enjoy unhindered. Eventually, we decided to return to Cape Town, our minds and cameras full of wonderful memories. On our descent, Aurora once again took to sitting to avoid looking over the side of the cable car. To her delight we reached ground level safely.

Once we were back in the car, we took the same route back to Bay View we had followed into Cape Town. It was as we saw once more the sign pointing in the direction of the Silver Mine that we decided to make a visit. I have to admit I went with caution, because I had spent my early life in the vicinity of a coal mine and felt nothing exciting in going to see a place which mined something thought to be more valuable than coal. As we drove along the track I imagined old gantries, disused wheels for raising and lowering cages and large piles of mining waste. What a surprise I got! I could not believe what we saw and why we had not ventured along this road before.

The site consisted of a beautiful lake around which the well-worn path followed the contours of the hills which encased it. We looked at each other in total amazement. It was beautiful. We parked the car and decided to walk along the path, oblivious to how the lake had come into being. We followed the lake path all the way round before following another path which took us up the slope and gave us an even better view of the lake and its surrounding landscape. We continued until we reached the point from which we could see the Atlantic stretching into the distance and Noordhoek beach, flat and appealing to the horsemen riding across it. When we reached the highest point we looked down into Hout Bay and re-lived the glorious sights we had enjoyed from Chapman's Peak. Somehow, I didn't see the pit tips around the Yorkshire coal mines giving such wonderful views, although Fitzwilliam had its moments.

It was the views which took our minds off the real purpose of the silver mine. Although we read about how it had once produced something of value, we could see nothing to give us a sense of what a mine looked like. I still see the high stacks of waste around my home village and others nearby, despite what the National Coal Board has done to try to conceal them. They remind me of the dust and dirt which caused my father's death and that of so many others, but here there was nothing to take us back to the days when this was a silver mine. It was a place of beauty and so impressed us that when we returned to Simons Town the following year, it was one of the first places we visited. The attraction of the glistening, quiet water of the lake remains a picture in our minds to this day, and I'm sure, no matter how many times we visited, we would still find it a place to enjoy because of its peaceful setting.

We had a further memorable experience in yet another of Cape Town's landmarks, a place so carefully manicured that it provided a different but equally beautiful episode in our South African adventures. Aurora's love of plants and flowers meant we had little chance of travelling to Cape Town without visiting Kirstenbosch Botanical Gardens. Even I was impressed by what we found as we made our way through the range of flora. The variety of plants and flowers was staggering and although there was, naturally enough, a concentration on those indigenous to South Africa, there were others which Aurora picked out and drew to my attention. But my favourite remained the Proteas, such a reminder of the great Springbok rugby sides of the days of Avril Malan and his contemporaries. I had watched the South Africans rugby team decimate England at Twickenham, and to be here in their native land, observing bush after bush of Proteas, one of the names I associated with the South African team, was beyond my dreams. The whole of the gardens were beautifully kept and provided an ideal location for the variety of sculptured figures, such as a mother and child and the indigenous animal, the impala, we came across. The large conservatory competed with the external gardens with its display of plants from different regions of the country – savanna, fynbos and karoo among others. But what the conservatory couldn't do was compete with the well grassed lawns of the Gardens. They were beautiful and tempting. It was here I decided to lie down in the hot sun and listen to the varied songs of the wide variety of birds which flitted from one bush to another. Eventually, I fell asleep and Aurora continued her tour.

Aurora awoke me before too long and we continued our wander through the gardens. There were signs directing us to different parts of the gardens, without which it would have been easy to get lost, but we were tempted by one in particular. It was a sign reading Skeleton Gorge. Who wouldn't be? But as we approached it we also read warnings of its dangers and how tourists looking to venture through the Gorge and up the incline towards Table Mountain had been attacked in recent months. Undeterred, we followed the path, crossed over another path where we saw reference to General Smuts, who it seems used this route a lot for his regular exercise, and climbed high above Kirstenbosch. When we turned and looked back in the direction of the Gardens we had a wonderful view of an area which was to become prized in future years as a World Heritage Site. Our joint opinion, as we look back at what we saw and photographed from that superb vantage point, was surprise that the Gardens had not been celebrated in this way long before 2004.

The lawns and flowers of the Gardens are not our only memory of Kirstenbosch. We were holidaying in Simons Town one Christmas when we read of an open air Christmas concert in the Gardens, which was to be given by the Cape Town Philharmonic. There is no doubt that the Kirstenbosch concerts were popular events and occurred throughout the year, but as we were in the area over Christmas it gave us the opportunity to celebrate in a special way. And so we booked and went.

The popularity of the concert was verified by the size of the audience. It was a hot, summer's day and most of the crowd were in shirt sleeves or light dresses and blouses, also with short sleeves. Many had brought their own chairs to sit on but more, including us, just sat on the dry grass looking down over the heads of others towards the conductor's rostrum. We had a good position and a good view of everything that happened on the stage. Aurora had prepared a small picnic tea for us and so we became one of several hundred, many with lunch boxes and drinks, who celebrated one part of Christmas Day in a special way.

The orchestra's high quality playing was supported by some first class solo singing. As usual, I became the critic. I had not played cornet and trumpet for so many years without paying special attention to others in different orchestras, especially the brass section. I couldn't find fault and simply lay back to enjoy. Aurora took some photographs of the orchestra and the singers and turned to photograph part of the audience. The photographs were records which would prompt the memory of that most pleasant occasion.

Once the concert was finished and we had wished those close to us a Merry Christmas, we made our way back to Simons Town to our bottle of champagne, the turkey and the Christmas cake Aurora had baked and brought with her from England. What better way to spend a Christmas than on a terrace as the warm sunshine gradually faded away to the West?

Chapter 16

The Winelands

Those warm, sunny days we spent in Simons Town over Christmas and the New Year took us away from the frost and snow of England. We knew we had to return, but that did not stop us enjoying South Africa. Only occasionally did the weather let us down. It wasn't rain or snow, but wind. Whereas in England the wind created snowdrifts, at the northern end of False Bay it created sand drifts. To us, it was an unusual experience to find roads blocked by sand but it happened during our stays on more than one occasion as we tried to travel from Simons Town by the road which rounded False Bay and opened up Hermanus, famous for whale watching, and the celebrated South African winelands. As for Hermanus, we went in the hope of seeing whales but came away disappointed. All we have to share with friends is the memory of a spout of water we took to be a whale as we travelled along the Cape Peninsular.

The experiences I am thinking about as I write are certainly more tangible. It was our intention to journey to the winelands, to Stellenbosch, Paarl and

Franchshoek, all three of which were reputed to be centres for good quality wine.

The route we had planned took us on the main road between the sea and the townships of Khayelitsha and Mitchels Plain. We had underestimated the wind, however. It came as a shock, therefore, when we discovered a police barricade across the road because of the sand drifts. The barricade prevented us taking the coastal road. We were forced to turn into Mitchells Plain, the coloured township which bordered the mainly Xhosa township of Khayelitsha. Once we had turned off the main road there were no diversion signs or anything else to help guide us through the streets of the township. I had to guess which roads to follow and which turns to take if we were to reach our destination. It reminded me of the journey we had made through the outskirts of Pretoria some months previously when we were lost in the dark. Here it was not dark, but as usual we had ringing in our heads the constant warnings from different receptionists and others about driving along unknown roads in certain parts of the country, and especially through townships.

Pretoria, Durban, Johannesburg, parts of Cape Town sprang to mind as cities in which we had been warned about dangers. Here we were in the middle of a township without any diversion signs and nothing to guide us. Even the map Aurora was holding did no more than show us the coastal road. Fortunately, and I don't know how, we managed to choose the correct directions without having to stop and ask, and although it sometimes meant stopping and doing a three point turn, or making a guess at a junction as to whether to turn left or right, we managed to get back to the main road. Despite the occasional heap of sand and the need to keep the windscreen wipers moving to clear the sand blown by the wind, we drove beyond the worst of the storm and the length of what was a very long coastal road before we began to climb towards our destination.

I was looking forward to visiting Stellenbosch with particular interest. In my days at school, when playing rugby was as important as learning history, I had come across the name of Danie Craven. I had read his book, 'Danie Craven on Rugby', and had been impressed by what he had to say. For me, he was one of the greats of South African rugby and as far as I was aware had established himself not only as a Springbok coach but as the coach at Stellenbosch University. He had certainly been a student there and his presence on the rugby field, either as scrum half or coach, resonated for me with the word Stellenbosch.

To visit the place with which he was so associated did not have the same impact on Aurora but when I added that his grandfather had been born, to my surprise, in the village of Steeton in Yorkshire, she showed a little more interest. I might add, little rather than more. But for me, the visit was to be more than a trip to the South African winelands. When I saw his statue by the university it reminded me so much of the statue of Webb Ellis which stands at the entrance to the town of Rugby in Warwickshire. It was Webb Ellis' picking up of a football at Rugby School which had started the great game and which gave it its name.

As we drove through the town, I recognised it bore all the marks of its recent history, with the white painted Dutch Reformed Church and the fine looking university buildings. It was also bordered by a township for the non-whites, which reflected the attitudes of the past, attitudes which had not yet totally disappeared. The comparison between the grand buildings of the university I had been keen to see and the dwellings in the township was more marked than I had dared to imagine. Though I could not surrender my admiration for Dr. Danie Craven, the rugby player, coach and scholar, I wondered how he had lived his life among such boundaries. I knew from my reading that he had made some efforts to overcome racism in rugby and no doubt would have been pleased to see that the best of the Springboks now include the best of the black Africans, but his good fortune in being white had clearly had an impact on what he had been able to achieve, both as a scholar and a rugby player.

I decided to park so that we could walk along the high street, see what the shops had to offer and have a coffee. We admired the white painted Dutch style houses and the mountainous surrounds of the town. Stellenbosch had more than a university and Danie Craven to celebrate. Wherever we looked beyond the town we could see vineyards and not surprisingly were tempted into one of the wineries by the roadside to taste the local produce. We managed to avoid buying any bottled wine, even though we were impressed by the aroma and the taste of the small samples we had been given, because we knew we had much further to drive and probably more wine to taste if we were to get a real sense of Western Cape's winelands.

Our next destination was Paarl, another of the famous wineland towns. We walked through the main streets a little but didn't stay long, attracted as we were out of the town by the glorious scenery which surrounded it. It was scenery we knew we would pass through as we followed our map and moved on towards Wellington and Bain's Kloof Pass. Our next port of call was to be Franschhoek; a town which we discovered had been washed in white. It seemed every house along every one of its calm streets was painted white.

Franschhoek is a fascinating town, one which my history teachers had failed to tell me about. They had taught my class about the Huguenots, the St Bartholomew Day Massacre of 1572 in France, the Edict of Nantes and its failure to sustain religious peace, and the eventual religious wars which led to the flight of the Huguenots from France in face of the severity with which they were being treated. Their disappearance robbed France of many of its most skilled citizens, whilst it added to those which offered a home to the refugees. We had learned about the Huguenots who came to England, settled in the south eastern counties and had a positive impact on the English economy, but it came as a surprise to hear that they had travelled to South Africa. They had been able to do this, apparently, with the aid of the Dutch East India Company.

When we reached Franschhoek, the evidence of the migrant Huguenots was everywhere. At the top of the high street, the three white pillars overlooking the pool and the paths bordered by white roses symbolise much of what the Huguenots believe. The three pillars represent the Holy Trinity, the lady statue holding a Bible reflects religious freedom, and the pool layed out in front represents the tranquility of mind and spiritual peace.

The memory of the first Huguenot settlers is further enhanced by the museum by the side of the memorial, which has remnants of the clothes and tools the earliest arrivals had with them. Many of the immigrants, we gathered, had become involved in farming, especially wine growing. I couldn't help but ask the same questions I was used to asking myself, a white skinned man, about apartheid. What would I, a Catholic, have done had I been faced with dealing with those who had different beliefs and refused to fall into line with the demands of the state? There was nothing in those symbols of goodness which was not present in my own Faith, but history has demonstrated there were occasions when those claiming to represent the Catholic Church had laid them aside and ignored their message. As I looked at the Huguenot memorial I wondered how I would have acted in those days of religious wars and persecution. As with apartheid, I hope I will never be tested!

From Franschhoek we journeyed through the mountains and vineyards to Robertson, another gem. It was here we decided we might as well carry on with our journey and stay overnight in a village called McGregor. We had heard of it when talking with friends before we left England and, being as close as we now were, it seemed a shame not to visit. We were not disappointed.

There were more white-washed houses, but they looked beautiful in the evening sunshine which had not yet hidden behind the surrounding hills. Here was another village cradled in vineyards and mountains.

We had no difficulty in finding somewhere to stay, a small traditional cottage just off the high street. It had all the amenities we needed for an overnight stay. We had an evening meal at the nearby restaurant and Aurora was able to buy enough as we walked around the village to make sure we had sufficient for breakfast.

The following morning we were up early enough to see children going to school, but not with their mothers in the four-by-four on what has become known in England as 'the school run'. Most were black and, as we had seen earlier in our travels, smartly dressed in school uniform. But again, we were aware they were seeking to save their shoes by carrying them along with the school bags they had over their shoulders. As we watched, we were unsure as to how far they would be walking.

It seemed amazing to us that so many lovely towns could have been built among rocks and mountains and had become so embedded that they now seemed to fit in a way which suggested the mountains and rocks had been built around them. Everything was so natural. The hills leading up to the mountain sides seemed to have been created for vines and the sun seemed destined to take up positions which guaranteed the annual ripening of the grapes. Nothing reflected the hard work it took for those who had laboured year after year to ensure the winelands produced the wine for which the area was famous.

A second night in the small cottage meant we could wander around the town, enjoy what it had to offer, and plan our return to Simons Town for the following day. It gave us the opportunity to visit the museum and to learn about the early settlers as well as about how the land had been developed.

The following day, we intended to take our time on the drive back to Simons Town, enjoy the scenery, and arrive at our flat before dark, hoping that the roads had been cleared of sand. It was not our intention to stop to buy wine, but we did. I bought half a dozen bottles of reasonable quality and then decided to splash out (as you will see later 'splash' is the appropriate word) on one bottle which, judging by the price, was of very good quality. I have to admit I tend to judge wine by its price, as I do with most things, especially as I'm not as good as some claim to be at circling the glass, sniffing the contents and then sipping before declaring the wine is good or bad. On this occasion, I put the bottles in the boot of the hire car and set off back towards our Bay View base.

We hadn't gone very far before I had to brake rather quickly. I heard what sounded like the clash of bottles in the boot and sensed a strong aroma of wine permeating the car. I tried to ignore Aurora's appeals to stop but the stronger the smell the more I realised I had to stop to see what had happened. The worst of my fears! The best bottle of wine, the most expensive, had smacked against the side of the boot and was in pieces. Wine, red and fragrant, (well it smelled like wine), was everywhere and the rear of the car was, dare I say, 'delightfully' full of the smell of a wine I had been looking forward to enjoying. If anyone had stopped to see what we were doing they may well have thought we were celebrating a great triumph rather than bewailing what was for me a terrible tragedy.

There was nothing more to do but to get rid of as much of the broken bottle as we could and try to mop up as much of the wine splashing about in the car boot, hoping that not too much had seeped into the carpet. We were to be disappointed. Even after Aurora had washed the car boot with soap and water when we were back at the flat, the scent of good quality wine persisted. As a result, we drove round for the rest of our holiday with the strong but appetising tang of wine in our nostrils, finding it a novel but enjoyable experience, hoping the South African police would not stop us and make assumptions about its source. No matter what we did we could not get rid of the smell of wine. Little wonder that when we returned the car a week later, the employees of the hire firm viewed the car with what looked like smiling faces.

Chapter 17

Robben Island

Before we left South Africa we knew there was one place above all which we had to visit. Robben Island, which had served as a prison for political prisoners and on which Nelson Mandela had been imprisoned until his release into house arrest in 1982, was a must.

The island lies just off the coast by Cape Town and like similar islands throughout the world, Alcatraz in the United States and Asinara in Sardinia, it provided, for many years, a secure place in which to keep law breakers and those who were regarded as dangerous to the state. We had read about Robben Island when we were on the Victoria and Alfred Waterfront and seen signs advertising the crossings to the Island. We decided to return to the harbour and make what was the most moving of the visits we had made throughout our time in South Africa.

The office for buying tickets for the crossing was adjoining the area of the harbour where we would board the boat. As we waited for the boat which would take us the short journey to the Island, we were able to look at the various photographs of the prison and some of the artistic work done by the prisoners. Among them were sketches drawn by Nelson Mandela when he was held on the Island – he had served eighteen years because of his opposition to white supremacy and the way the majority of his fellow countrymen had been treated.

To the apartheid government, Mandela was a notorious opponent and their hope was that a long sentence on the Island would see him lose his support in South Africa and especially in the township of Soweto where he lived. With luck, he would become a forgotten man. As we were to learn on our visit to the prison, it didn't quite work out that way. In fact, it appears Mandela became as much a problem on the Island as he had been off it.

We boarded the boat which was to take us across the narrow strait to the Island. We had heard that the crossing could be a 'bit bouncy' but neither of us was concerned as we took seats at the front of the boat, hoping to get an early view of the Island. I had crossed the English Channel in gales without the problem of sea sickness and so felt confident that I would manage this crossing without difficulty. Aurora was of the same mind. Whether it was because we chose to sit at the front or not I don't know, but for me the crossing became something of a nightmare. The rise and fall of the boat did its damage, especially as I saw the sea one second and not the next. By the time we reached the Island I felt pretty sick. Once off the boat, thank goodness, I felt much better – that seems to be how sea sickness works.

We were guided around the prison, as was the custom, by a former inmate. He was tall and, not surprisingly, black. He was obviously used to taking touring parties around and his personal experience on the Island ensured he could speak with some authority. He pointed out important landmarks such as the white painted garrison church, the leper cemetery from the days when the Island was a leper colony, the watch tower and the gated entrance to the prison. He pointed along the coast of the Island, saying there was a small village, mainly inhabited by ex-prisoners and guards, further down the Island.

Once inside the prison he took us along a corridor of cells, indicating the one in which Mandela had spent his 18 years. Mandela had been imprisoned in 1964 because of his resistance to the policies of the Government, and he stayed in prison and house arrest until his release in 1990 – 1991. It was during our visit that we learned he was not on Robben Island through all the years of his incarceration. He had experienced other prisons on the mainland.

When Mandela was on the Island he was, as were the other prisoners, confined to a small cell. It was cramped and contained no more than bed clothes, which were on the stone floor rather than a bed, a small table not much higher than a stool and a bucket for toilet necessities. All the other cells revealed similar characteristics.

Having shown us the living conditions, our guide led us outside where we saw the walled square where prisoners used to work with hammer and chisel and the lime quarry, in which he said Mandela had to work on occasions and which was the least popular and most dangerous of the work given to the prisoners. He then took us into the library, which contained only a few books, but one on display, Shakespeare's Julius Caesar, bore an ink mark made by Mandela.

Our guide had been in prison at the same time as Mandela and was happy to describe to us the life they led. He talked about the hardship and the rigour of prison life and of how badly they were treated on occasions by the guards. But he also spoke about the periods of pleasure, when the prisoners had their annual half-hour visit from a friend, received their six-monthly letter, were allowed to spend some time in the library and were allowed to play football. He added that throughout his time in prison, Mandela had been seen as the leader, the man to go to with a problem, the man who could influence the guards. 'He showed himself to be the man who had the qualities that were to make him the President he became,' our guide said with obvious pride. He said he invariably led fellow prisoners to do the opposite to what the guards demanded. 'If the guards said, 'Quick march,' Mandela would say, 'Slow march,' and if the guards said, 'Left turn,' Mandela would say, 'Right turn,' and the prisoners would follow.'

It was as we were leaving and we were all expressing our gratitude for the care our guide had taken with us that Aurora said to him, 'Can I ask a question?' The words sounded alarm bells for me because I know every time she said the same to me there was going to be a question that I would find difficult to answer. She had already managed to disturb our host in Graaff Reinet with a similar approach. The guide, in his innocence, simply said, 'Yes.' He was then asked the unanswerable for a man who had spent a good deal of his life in prison on a small island. 'Have you ever been to a prison in Eastern Europe?'

Not surprisingly he answered 'No, I've never had any reason.' His quizzical expression, however, revealed much more. Then the killer punch. 'Well I'll tell you. This is like a holiday camp compared to what used to happen to our political prisoners. Most of them we never saw again.' It was time for me to steer Aurora away and over to the boat as the startled look on the guide's face was mirrored by those on the faces of other visitors who had overhead the conversation. Aurora was un-phased. She had felt it important to suggest there were worse places to be than Robben Island.

On our journey back to Cape Town, Aurora continued to express her opinions to me about the differences between Robben Island and her knowledge of what had happened to political prisoners in her own country during communist times, a conversation which took my mind off any thought of sea sickness. She talked of the prisons which were built so that the communists could re-educate those they felt were not in line with their own values. It was only years later that Romanians, freed from the shackles of communism, learned about what had been happening to their countrymen. 'The communists tried to get rid of a whole generation so that a new generation, and I was part of it, could be brought up in the way they wanted. You can't believe what we've learned since Ceausescu went. The different horrific tortures designed to destroy personality, the substitution of faeces for the Blessed Sacrament, the beatings prisoners endured, the hours and days they spent without sleep, and the particularly punishing torture of the prisoners walking for hours on their hands and knees.' Aurora shook her head, gritted her teeth and closed her eyes as she tried to drive the visions from her mind. 'They even allowed doctors in to experiment on the prisoners as they tried to rob people of one personality and give them another. And the prisoners were from all different backgrounds – professionals, priests, workers – you name it and they were there. They even forced prisoners to torture one another. When they died, they disappeared, and to this day families don't know what happened to their loved ones.'

She went on to describe how an escapee managed to get to the BBC and how the subsequent publicity caused panic. Panic of such magnitude that those who had been involved in controlling the prisoners – doctors, psychiatrists, guards – had to be prevented from revealing what they had done and so, along with the prisoners, many were executed and buried in mass graves. Little wonder she had made her comment about Robben Island and a holiday camp! But neither of us knew the full story of those who spent a good proportion of their lives on the Island and I have no doubt none of us would have wanted to be in their place.

She herself had been closely questioned by the Securitate on several occasions, a lamp shone in her eyes and bullied into telling what she was prepared to say, simply because she was a travel guide and took visitors from Western Europe around to see the important sights in her country. The Securitate were suspicious of anyone who came into contact with westerners and were keen to prevent any non-communist ideas penetrating the country they controlled. They were particularly alert to the occasions when Aurora met up with the Italian Ambassador and he passed a book on to her. The book was confiscated and Aurora warned of the danger of her undermining the Government of her country.

My own experience of communism and its implications for those who resisted the principles and policies on which it was based extended to a visit to Russia in 1968, when I had a view across the River Neva of the Peter and Paul Fortress in St. Petersburg and the stories I heard subsequently of the gulags in Siberia. *'Fortunately,'* I thought, *'Habeas Corpus still rules in the United Kingdom'*.

When we arrived back at the Victoria and Alfred we had another look around the small museum dedicated to the artistic work done by prisoners. We knew we had to have a genuine memory of Nelson Mandela, and so we bought a small booklet, 'my robben island', in which he had drawn a few sketches portraying aspects of his life in prison. We had seen the authentic barred window, the lighthouse, the church, and we had also seen his cell. All were portrayed in the booklet by Mandela's unskilled hand, but it's the sort of sketch book you keep forever. In its own way it reminds us of what Mandela suffered for so many years, and the sacrifices countless black citizens of South Africa were prepared to make as they sought to win equality.

As I look back on those few years during which I was closely involved with educational change in South

Africa I think I have found the answer to the scratching of my head and wondering why I might want to write a book about South Africa. Everybody has heard of Nelson Mandela and everybody I meet talks very highly of him. They refer to his commitment to a cause, to his willingness to sacrifice his own freedom for the countrymen who were so badly treated and to his willingness to forgive when the right time came. My sentiments are with them, and strongly, but during my time in South Africa I met others across the nine Provinces who will never command the same attention or be thought of in the same way. As he did, they worked hard to change the face of South Africa, seeking to bring equal opportunities to its varied population. Many risked everything for the same cause. I put among those Todd Masilela, his immediate family and his brothers, to whom I am proud to dedicate this book.